T

Bou **ack**

Time to Bounce Back

How to heal and move on from the pandemic

By

Barbara Dewast

Time to Bounce Back - How to heal and move on from the pandemic by Barbara Dewast

Published by the Author, as Director of Darebe Ltd Company number 12167983

www.barbaradewast.com

Cover by Lauren Squillino

ISBN: 9798825566306

Printed in the UK

1st Edition

Contents

This book is for you if...

If you feel this pandemic has affected you in an unprecedented way,

If you feel an urge to slow down,

If you would like to reflect on how you have been impacted by this period, and

If the time feels right to explore how to progress on your journey in a more mindful and purposeful way.

I am a mother of 3, a wife, a friend, a sister, a daughter and a leadership and life coach. During the Covid-19 pandemic, I've been working with individuals, groups and teams navigating the unprecedented levels of change. I've also been holding the emotions in my own heart, in my children's lives, in my romantic life as well as with my friends and family. It's been WOAH - to say the least!! A journey - heavy at times, with tears and pain, disappointments, fears, and also with unexpected joy, fun, laughter and a lot of love.

Throughout this pandemic, I've observed how the world around me has been affected, each and everyone of us at different levels, and to different depths. I feel no one has been left intact. No one. I am writing this book as I believe that before we rush back into our busy lives, before we try to put behind us the impact that the pandemic has had on us, we should pause. We should take the time to observe how we have been impacted, acknowledge any shifts, good and bad, heal any bruises, self-care, and then we can bounce back, start afresh, in a healthy, stable and more balanced world.

My values of compassion, self-love, care and generosity feed through this reflection. I work and live in central London, where efficiency, high intellect and rational thinking is king - although I value and thrive in this world, I want to encourage slowing down and self-care, that in turn will bring more happiness and fulfilment in our lives.

The pain involved with the process of self-examination can be considerable. I want to honour the respect, and love that you need to have for yourself, for your life, for who you are as a person - to take a deep look at yourself. You'll need to invest some courage in the process if you are to look into your emotions and understand what is getting in the way of your balance, your potential and your happiness. I want to acknowledge that this takes energy, and it requires bravery. Not everyone will be ready to do this, and that's absolutely fine. But you should also know that the day that you are ready to undergo this process is probably the ideal time to begin a healing journey.

Once we heal, a world of possibilities opens up, our perspectives shift, we see potential, opportunity and choice.

Throughout this book I've used real life examples, of my clients, my community and my family. I have, for confidentiality reasons, amended the names and some of the external circumstances. The message is intact and all experiences shared are real.

As you read the book, I invite you to have a notebook handy to take notes, or even to write in this book. It's meant to be a reflective place, and I encourage you to make it yours. To write, doodle or whatever is needed to allow you to feel and think deeply.

Part I
Acknowledging what is here

1. For me - Barbara

My grandmother died in the middle of the Covid-19 pandemic.

She didn't die due to the virus that created a global health crisis, or complications associated with it. My grandmother died because it was her time. In many ways, she was ready to leave. She had lived a full life and reached the venerable age of 92.

As she lay on her deathbed, she had her two daughters close to her. They held her hands as her gentle heart gradually stopped beating, and she serenely passed on into the next life. She was at peace with her existence in this world. She had closed the circle of this mortal coil and had nothing left to give or glean from it.

I was fully aware of this, but losing her was still a profoundly upsetting experience. A few weeks passed and the sadness and grief were still circulating within my internal systems, as nostalgic images of times that we'd spent together lingered in my consciousness. I was still living with the scars and bruising of her loss.

Thankfully, I know from my profession that dealing with grief takes time. It isn't something that can be simply brushed away. There is a healing process and we all have to go through it. There is no other possible way of negotiating this.

However, beneath the pain and sadness of my grandmother's departure, I could also perceive something deeper. It felt stronger and longer. It wasn't clear where it began or ended, like a thread. And I realised that it was more than just losing someone who had meant so much to me. What I was feeling was a form of post-pandemic grief.

The more that I considered this, the more that it made sense. I contemplated the almost unimaginable level of grief that people had experienced in a short space of time. Sorrow was almost hanging in the air, like an unpleasant aroma. It was tangible. My grandmother's death was part of the way that I felt, but there was something much bigger at the heart of it. The weight of everything that I'd been through, that my clients had been through and that society had been through since March 2020, was bearing down on me. Every part of me needed to heal from this torrid time. My body and mind needed to heal. My heart needed to heal. My senses needed to heal. My soul needed to heal.

"Healing isn't a linear process - we move two steps forward and one step back (...) Committing to the practices of healing is the first step. Be patient with

yourself, get support where you can, and positive changes will occur without you even noticing."[1].

There is no doubt that the Covid-19 pandemic and the related lockdowns have created a degree of change that is unprecedented in living memory. On a global level it has resulted in the biggest impact on people's lives since the Second World War. The more I investigated the issue, the more I realised that the whole scenario had enacted an immense impact on our collective psyche. It's not surprising then that the mental health charity Mind's survey discovered that more than half of adults (60%) and over two-thirds of young people (68%) indicated that their mental health deteriorated during the March 2020 lockdown[2].

And as my investigation into this subject unfolded, it became obvious that this was a particularly important issue. This was arguably as significant as Covid-19 itself. For myself, everything was thrown up in the air, and when the pieces fell back to the ground they were naturally a little jumbled up. As a woman, as a mother, as a professional, my existence felt rather uncertain, not to mention those of my immediate family; the people who are closest to me.

---

[1] Healing Is the New High: A Guide to Overcoming Emotional Turmoil and Finding Freedom, 2021 by Vex King Hay House UK. p14

[2] Mind. (2020). The mental health emergency: How has the coronavirus pandemic impacted our mental health? https://www.mind.org.uk/media-a/5929/the-mental-health-emergency_a4_final.pdf?

But it went deeper than that. I could empathise profoundly with the worry of others, with the pain that people were going through. There is a line in a Radiohead song - *rows of houses are bearing down on me* - and that is precisely how I felt. I could sense the weight, the fear and sadness of people all over the world. It felt heavy, to say the least.

We are all different when it comes to empathy, compassion and feeling emotion for others. As a coach, I have trained myself to listen, to feel and to hold what is felt out there; naturally being empathetic is part of my remit. But I have equally learned not to hold negative emotions inside me, to release them and constantly refresh my emotional state. This is a critically important part of being an effective coach.

I recognised that this overarching emotion of fear and anxiety did not belong to me, or certainly did not belong to me alone. I found it particularly challenging to overcome these deep sensations of suffering, as I could see, feel, perceive this grief and wounding with great clarity around me. This is the first part of the process involved with healing and moving forward, acknowledging what is here.

The fear of illness and of contaminating one another has taken a terrible toll on us mentally. The fear of the other has almost morphed into agoraphobia, as people have been confined over this extended period. Some people have been more fortunate than others. I myself have a very close-knit family, and we were able to recover from the situation fairly rapidly, as we were able to support one another. My close family is spread over France, Northern and Central Africa, and Germany - so we had already been accustomed to supporting one another for many years, while living in different countries. Being connected, supportive, making time and sharing experiences are qualities that we've been training to acquire for quite some years.

During the Covid-19 lockdowns, I observed other people developing the same ability, managing to connect and keep close even despite the hurdles put in their way. I was part of this process - I've celebrated weddings, birthdays and evening drinks online like never before! Don't get me wrong; this is not what I wished for the world. But it did help during this tough time. I even noticed that some friendships took root and grew during the pandemic, taking more space than ever before. It became important for me to allow for daily time on the phone to share, support and connect with my inner circle. With my husband and my three children, relations were strained at times, but I also observed our relationship grow closer. My children played together more frequently, and our family time occupied a more privileged space. I noticed this new and indulgent bubble of emotional sustenance with other similar families as well.

Nonetheless, Covid-19 has taken its toll on our collective psyche, severely limiting the spectrum of normal human emotion. There has been an absence of joy. A dearth of spontaneity. A lack of beauty. This will have a diverse array of consequences all over the globe. But, for me, I feel an urge to connect with people. It feels as if I have been chained up to some extent. My world has contracted around me; when I want it to be bigger, to be about discovery and excitement.

When I recognise this sensation, I also feel great empathy for others who were less fortunate than me, who had less space, no loved ones around them to ease the ennui, or both. And then I also felt an urge to move on, to move forward, to put this regrettable period behind me, behind all of us.

Another major issue arose when, later during the pandemic, I contracted Covid. I had been careful, like most people, but after 18 months of isolation and online calls, I was ready to see my clients face-to-face again. Unfortunately, it was not long before I fell ill. This was an unpleasant period; it was a full 10 days of being quite feverish and fighting all sorts of strange symptoms - sweat, fever, breathing difficulties, etc. I also remember feeling a deep sense of sadness when I lost my sense of taste and smell. I love food, I love cooking and I enjoy the smell of a soft candle in the evening. It felt that all of this had been taken away from me, and somehow this cut deeper and affected me even more than the physical symptoms. I was forced to isolate in the upstairs of my house, leaving my husband to manage the children. They eventually left for summer holidays without me. The fear of spreading the virus was too strong; I had to sit it out. And I did. But this was not a particularly happy time!

As the summer progressed, I took great care to look after myself diligently, to eat the most fresh and colourful food possible, to sleep and follow all of the guidance that was provided by doctors and scientists And, slowly but surely, I started to emerge and feel better. This improved sense of state endured for quite a while, but then symptoms of long Covid-19 began to emerge - dyspnea, loss of hair and tiredness. That's when I realised that the pandemic was not over. I could sense my body fighting back against the virus and the long term symptoms which had a negative impact on my mood, general well-being and energy.

Going through this made me realise how tough it must have been for other people who experienced similar symptoms, in their own unique circumstances. I see myself as mentally resilient, I have been blessed with a happy childhood and a beautiful trauma-less life so far, and I regularly process and take care of my mental health - but I have still witnessed how difficult dealing with all of this has been for me. I am just one example of many, and I feel the multiplication of the many makes this a real social, global pain, and a massive wound to heal.

The desire to write this book emerged as I realised that even if I did not have a specific cure for the bruises and hardships that I'd endured during the pandemic, I had extensive experience in dealing with emotions, with change, with fear and with the unsettling feeling of uncertainty. Combined with my natural inclination to be with people, to listen and to empathise, I have gathered tools, tricks and tips that have helped me navigate what has been a punishing period of my life. I believe that we are all on a journey, that no one has everything figured out, but that we are all trying to find the best and most authentic path for ourselves through life, and balance all of the multitude of challenges, opportunities and experiences that are inevitably thrown at us along the way...

Through my ongoing coaching work, I have coached clients for thousands of hours, helping people achieve clarity regarding what is important for them, identifying the obstacles that are getting in their way, and crafting a plan on how to move forward. This is achieved via a thought-triggering process, and by building a genuine and mutual relationship of trust. I help my clients to gain confidence that pertains to their particular values, helping them to identify what they wish to stand up for in life, and, equally importantly, what they no longer want to be part of their lives.

I have accompanied many people through changes, through gruelling hardships, and helped them find their way. We acknowledge what is here, the baggage that accompanies them at all times through life - I refer to this as their 'suitcases' - and then we explore how to build the resilience and energy required to pick them up and help them to move forward in life. Within the pages of this book, my intention is to do exactly this for the reader - to acknowledge what is here, for me, for you and for our communities, to honour our bruises and pain, and then to pause, to reflect and gradually recharge, so that we can find the energy to bounce back effectively. I strongly believe that if we bounce back too quickly then we run the risk of functioning erratically, running out of fuel, and losing our sense of direction.

The second part of this book encourages you to slow down - to create some space, to think, reflect and let things be. By being fully present with ourselves, we increase our ability to be more thoughtful and purposeful when we, at last, feel ready to move again. In the third and final section we will see how to bounce back and move on in our lives in a deliberate and thoughtful way. We will explore how to nurture our energy, emotions and navigate the journey of our lives.

2. For you - The reader

The bruises I've seen...

As a coach, I've naturally encountered many people who have accrued significant mental stress during the Covid-19 era. Still today, even if we've been living with the illness for a while, I often feel and perceive that there is a lot of bruising out there. I've seen a great deal of sadness and pain, partly from illness, but also, and mostly, from isolation, fear, and the lack of control that people have had over the situation, which has inevitably led to a draining sense of uselessness.

Intensity of the System

Connection and disconnection is another key dichotomy here. As the pandemic has unfolded, there has been almost a mania to be connected to the news. Understandably, people wanted to gain access to all of the latest data - how many positive Covid-19 cases have emerged, how many people have died, how busy hospitals have become, and all of the other chilling numbers that were coming in on a daily basis. People connected themselves to all of this suffering in quite a deep fashion, and when this was in their consciousness all of the time it rapidly became overwhelming.

Even if you didn't follow the news every day, you might still have found it difficult to escape the enormity of the situation. For example, I remember seeing my phone, and I had over 200 messages at one time in the space of a few hours. I was being hugely connected to a situation that was almost entirely defined by negative energy. It all builds up; the pressure builds up both internally and externally.

When I was working with clients, a lot of the work was taking place via screens on video calls. I was spending 7-8 hours a day, sometimes even more, connected to that as well. Suddenly, not deliberately and through no fault of my own, I found myself in a position of being continually connected, continually observed and needing to be continually responsive. This was definitely not a new behaviour, but the intensity of the situation had increased beyond a level that had even been imaginable previously.

By now, most of us know what it means to be hyper-connected. We've all been in this state during the Covid-19 situation. And the benefits of disconnecting, unplugging and silencing the relentless din of our technological culture, is so valuable.

Isolated

What is also important in the Covid-19 scenario is the prominent position that fear has occupied. Those who have been glued to their newsfeed have absorbed nothing less than a constant diet of fear. And it's not just the media - friends, family, our peers, the government, the medical establishment; everyone has been the bearer of repeated bad news. Fear has been predominant in the communication and discourse surrounding Covid, and this fear has been festering away, unchecked, unimpeded, until it has grown to a magnitude that feels decidedly unhealthy.

Coupled with this fear has been the restraint of freedom. It's very important to acknowledge this. Seeking freedom is part of our human identity - history is the best testimonial for this. Over centuries, we have repeatedly fought for our freedom. So to have this removed completely will naturally take a terrible toll on our sense of well-being. If we take the concepts of fear and removal of freedom, it's clear that when the two are coupled, it's not a state in which most people are likely to thrive, or even tread water. It has been a hugely limiting and constricting experience, and we won't recover from this for quite some time.

There are several aspects to his lack of human contact, but often we overlook the most basic and fundamental. Literal human contact, touching another person, is a profound human need. Extensive research supports this assertion, leaving us no doubt that if we remove the ability to touch and be touched from someone, the psychological well-being and mental health of that person is highly likely to diminish.

A close friend, Taylor, was unable to stay with his newborn baby at the postnatal clinic of a hospital. This was an incredibly difficult few days for him and his new family. While fathers were most of the time able to attend births during the pandemic, they were asked, during a few months in 2020 and again 2021, to leave the hospital immediately afterwards. As a result, babies have lacked the physical skin to skin contact with their dads, in these intense and precious bonding days. This also meant that many women that gave birth were shorn of contact with their partners at challenging times. They may have had a Caesarian section and be required to stay in hospital, yet be deprived of the sort of human connection and support that is especially required post birth.

Studies indicate that touch activates the body's vagus nerve, leading to the release of oxytocin, and, consequently, positive sensations. Research conducted by James Coan, Hillary Schaefer and Richard Davidson found that people were less inclined to feel stress in a challenging situation when a romantic partner stroked their arm[3]. Even a simple handshake can help to lower cortisol and reduce stress, thanks to the release of oxytocin; often described as the 'happiness' or 'loving' hormone.

Our predilection for touch is built into our evolutionary biology. Our closest relations in the animal kingdom, non-human primates, spend as much as 20% of the average day grooming one another[4]. Thus, the benefits of touch begin from the tenderest age; a review of academic literature by Dr. Tiffany Field found that preterm newborns who received just three 15-minute sessions of touch therapy each day for 5-10 days gained 47% more weight than premature infants who'd received standard medical treatment[5].

So when human contact is removed from our everyday existence, the consequences can be quite severe. One story I encountered that is illustrative of this was of a gentleman, Etienne, who had surgery during the pandemic. It was open-heart surgery, so it was an operation of the utmost seriousness, but thankfully he pulled through. There were some complications which

---

[3] Coan, J., Schaefer, H. & Davidson, R. (2006). *Lending a hand: social regulation of the neural response to threat*. Psychological Science, 2006 Dec; 17(12), pp. 1032-9

[4] Dunbar, R. (2012). *Bridging the bonding gap: the transition from primates to humans*. Philosophical Transactions of the Royal Society B: Biological Sciences, 2012 Jul 5; 367(1597), pp. 1837–1846.

[5] Field, T. (2010). *Touch for socioemotional and physical well-being: A review*. Developmental Review, Volume 30, Issue 4, December 2010, pp. 367-383.

meant that he had to spend a brief sojourn in hospital, but the surgery was ultimately successful. It must have been a gigantic relief.

But he was confined to a hospital bed when the virus was circulating at its most rapid rate. This was the height of the pandemic. And, unfortunately, as he was attempting to recover from his major surgery, he contracted the Covid-19 virus. Suddenly, he found himself being transported from the recovery ward for heart surgery straight into the Covid-19 wing of the hospital. And his life hung in the balance once more.

This situation was challenging enough in itself, but the lines of communication were also never satisfactorily opened. No-one told his family. And then once he was sequestered in the Covid-19 ward, he wasn't allowed any visitors. His loved ones went from worrying about a serious and life-threatening surgery to being locked away from contact with him, at a time when there was still no guarantee that he would pull through. They literally knocked on the door of the ward, only to be turned away without contact, while the gentleman was crying with anguish the whole time. Any form of direct contact was forbidden by law. His family were permitted merely 20 minutes to speak with him via a single shared tablet for the whole ward.

Meanwhile, his condition deteriorated. His symptoms went from bad to worse. And he sadly passed away. He was never afforded the opportunity to bid farewell to his loved ones. They were taken completely out of the loop and denied all contact, at a time when every fibre of their being yearned to be with him. It must have been unbelievably painful and stressful for everyone involved.

The story resonated with people in France, where the situation unfolded. The injustice and sheer suffering of the situation struck people in their hearts. It prompted a huge petition online - signed by 48,000 people[6] - which essentially communicated the view that societally, we were acquiescing with scenarios that are wholly unacceptable. That would never have been permitted in any other situation. Whatever the rights and wrongs, whatever your view might be, I find it is extremely difficult to defend a dying man not being allowed to be with his family during the final moments of his life.

---

[6]https://www.change.org/p/le-droit-de-visite-aux-patients-et-personnes-%C3%A2g%C3%A9es-doit-%C3%AAtre-reconnu-pour-tous-%C3%A0-tout-moment-de-l-hospitalisation-quel-que-soit-le-contexte-sanitaire

The Impact of Isolation

I also worked with many clients who were shut away, isolated, and lonely. This had all manner of mental, emotional and psychological consequences. For example, Billy, a client of mine, is a gentleman in his eighties. He's a very wise and smart man, still very involved, serving as the chairman of an active charity in the North of England. He also does a lot of gardening and certainly keeps himself busy in usual circumstances.

However, the pandemic had a profound impact on him. It floored him. He was more fragile medically than most people because of his age, and definitely more vulnerable. As a consequence, his daughter was only allowed to visit him once per week. And even when she was able to see him, she was forced to don a mask and gloves, and wasn't allowed to be in the same room as him. It felt deeply impersonal and he became isolated.

After a few months of this, he confided in me one day. *"Barbara, I'm afraid of people. I'm scared to just go in the streets and talk to people."* This was a man who was previously sociable and full of life, yet he had been reduced to a shadow of himself. I felt powerless and sad as his growing sense of agoraphobia took over.

This is particularly important, as there can be a tendency to dismiss, or at least diminish, the impact and importance of reduced social contact. We can drink, sleep, breathe and survive without social contact, but the vast majority of us cannot prosper, as reflected in the research of renowned American psychologist Professor Martin Seligman. This pioneering psychologist is best-known for his work focused on positive psychology - and for creating his PERMA model; an acronym that comprises five key elements of psychological and emotional well-being, namely positive emotion, engagement, relationships, meaning and achievement[7]. For Seligman, positive emotions inevitably emanate from desirable social circumstances, and life outcomes follow on from this. Should you want to dig deeper and get clarity as to what brings you joy, and positive thoughts or feelings, and areas you might want to focus more on.

There is a wealth of scientific evidence that underlines both the importance of social contact, and also the mental and physical impact if it is withdrawn for an extended period. Psychologist Susan Pinker has commented that direct contact with other people is essential, as it triggers parts of our nervous system that release a "whole cascade of neurotransmitters", which regulate responses to stress and anxiety[8].

As early as 1965, an extensive study of 7,000 people in California concluded that "people who were disconnected from others were roughly three times more

---

[7] Madeson, M. (2021). *Seligman's PERMA+ Model Explained: A Theory of Wellbeing.* Positive Psychology.
[8] National Public Radio. (2020). *Susan Pinker: What Makes Social Connection So Vital To Our Well-Being?.*

likely to die...than people with strong social ties"[9]. The physical reasons for this have also been documented. People chronically lacking in social contact are at risk of elevated levels of stress and inflammation, and these, in turn, can impact negatively on every bodily system and organ.

In fact, research suggests that the physical impact of loneliness can be just as serious as the most notorious health conditions. A 1988 study published in the Science journal indicated that "social isolation is on a par with high blood pressure, obesity, lack of exercise or smoking as a risk factor for illness and early death.[10]"

Reduced social interaction can also damage mental health. Dr. Emma Seppala, of the Stanford Center for Compassion and Altruism Research and Education, wrote that "people who feel more connected to others have lower levels of anxiety and depression. Moreover, studies show they also have higher self-esteem, greater empathy for others, are more trusting and cooperative and, as a consequence, others are more open to trusting and cooperating with them."

---

[9] 7. Berkman, Lisa, F. & Syme, S., Leonard. (1979). *Social Networks, Host Resistance and Mortality: A Nine-Year Follow-Up Study of Alameda County Residents.* American Journal of Epidemiology, Volume 109, Issue 2, February 1979, pp. 186–204.

[10] House J. S., Landis K. R. & Umberson D. (1988). *Social relationships and health. Science 241, pp. 540–545.*

Seppala concluded by noting that "social connectedness generates a positive feedback loop of social, emotional and physical well-being"[11]. This was corroborated by recent research published in The Lancet, which found that social isolation is associated with increased instances of depression and anxiety[12].

The whole notion of the importance of strong social relationships was perhaps first expressed by the American psychologist Abraham Maslow. In his 1943 paper "A Theory of Human Motivation" in the journal Psychological Review, Maslow established social belonging and interaction as a critical pillar of well-being.[13] Ever since this central plank of Maslow's work was published, extensive scientific research and study have repeatedly consolidated this impression.

Thus, there are potentially huge mental, emotional, psychological and physical consequences of social isolation. No matter how robust you may appear, or believe yourself to be, no-one is immune from this.

---

[11] Seppala, Dr., E. (2014). *Connectedness & Health: The Science of Social Connection. Stanford Center for Compassion and Altruism Research and Education.*

[12] Newman, M., G. & Zainal, N., H. (2020). *The value of maintaining social connections for mental health in older people.* The Lancet Volume 5, Issue 1.

[13] Maslow, A. (1943). *A Theory of Human Motivation. Psychological Review 50, pp. 370-96.*

Process

In coaching, an important part of the work that I do with my clients is referred to as 'process'. This aspect is about working with your emotions, so that you can understand what is present for you in your life. Also importantly, it's the impact that this has on you, and what you are tolerating as a result during every day of your life.

"We'll hit a point when we will have to deal with it in a different way, and process the fear that this experience might have filled us with[14]".

The first step of 'process' is acknowledging what is here - 'naming' it. Then we explore the issue, diving deep into the emotion or wound that exists. We examine this through words, metaphors and resonance. We allow the emotion to take over. We connect with all our senses, allowing colours, smells, textures, words, noise to define this pain, this bruise, and, gradually, magic happens. The mind shifts and we begin to find a way to climb up out of the emotion, allowing ourselves to move forward in life. This is a process that I believe most of us will need to go through when it comes to pandemic grief. Before we can forge a positive direction in life, we need to understand how the pandemic and its related consequences have affected us, our loved ones, our work and our livelihoods,

---

[14] King, V. (2021). Healing Is the New High: A Guide to Overcoming Emotional Turmoil and Finding Freedom, pp. 270. Hay House UK.

so that we can move forward with our lives purposefully and productively.

I've graphed out the various steps of process, and invite you to follow them one at a time at the end of this section.

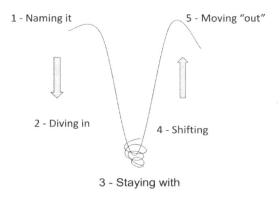

1 - Naming it   5 - Moving "out"

2 - Diving in   4 - Shifting

3 - Staying with

Right in the middle of the pandemic, things were not going well for Emilie, a friend of mine. She was suffering from a form of long Covid, with severe physical and mental consequences. We agreed to conduct a coaching session, in an attempt to support her through this difficult patch. Part of this session was a "process exercise", which involved examining her wounds deeply, so that we could gain an awareness of what she was dealing with.

We both closed our eyes, and explored her wounds using metaphors, feelings, and emotions, ensuring that we were truly curious as we explored. We did not try to fix or judge what was there; instead, we focused on increasing her awareness of what was there for her. As we explored, she told me that she could sense a painful ball in her neck, which felt spiky. And every time that she moved her neck, she could feel the spikes moving inside her - that brought tears of pain, of anger and frustration. Every day, she was living with that nagging sensation within her throat, invisible to the rest of the world, but intensely palpable for her. Through the process of our practice, we connected with it, acknowledged its existence, and Emilie found it liberating to be able to finally recognise what was there, and what it felt like.

Awareness is critically important. Only when we've become fully aware of our situation, of our feelings and emotions, can we learn to accept them, to live with them, or to grow, and change what is possible for us. Awareness is curative, it's the first step to a healing process, physically and emotionally. In this respect, I strongly encourage cultivating more self-awareness. For some it will take time, acknowledging, connecting with the pain again and again, until slowly it starts to ease, the body and the mind starts to accept it and to make space for it. It will then hurt less, be less intense. It takes courage, self-love, acceptance, and patience.

Considering the hectic pace of modern life, many of us have a tendency to bustle through our lives, without properly reflecting on who we are, or even fully understanding what we want out of life. Thus, exercises that cultivate more self-awareness can be really valuable. If we are able to observe and accurately identify our thoughts, feelings and impulses, and determine whether they are grounded in reality or not, we are far more likely to make sound life decisions and lead a healthier life both psychologically and physically. A valuable part of this process can be conducting a core values review, in order to improve self-knowledge and help cultivate a life that reflects these values.

I find that it is very difficult to achieve positive outcomes in life if you've failed to satisfactorily address your wounds. So I am here today encouraging my clients, my loved ones, and the world around me to reflect on their bruises and acknowledge what is here for them, so that they can heal. I strongly believe that we're not going to ultimately feel better by simply ploughing forward and ignoring the impact the pandemic has had on us. We need to pause and reset. And the first part of this process is self-examination. Be brave and creative. Take a deep dive into your own space. Follow the steps below, just be curious, don't judge, and let your creativity speak for itself.

The pandemic has been particularly difficult. And this whole saga has consequences. People are bruised. This may take on different shapes, colours and identities depending on the individual, but most people carry with them the bruising that the pandemic has created.

Processing you

On to you. I invite you to take some time to do the work on yourself. For some it will be smooth and fairly accessible exercise, for others it might be a very sensitive, and even painful experience. Feelings and emotions tell us something, listen to them, be curious, open and they will move. In essence we will examine what is difficult, what we are struggling to be with. So know that this process exercise requires a safe space, a lot of self-love, along with patience and courage to be truthful to yourself.

Coming back to the curve we saw previously, I invite you to start in 1, on the left hand side and to move down and up into the curve. As you progress through the curve, you might want to close your eyes to allow your thoughts to expand, or you might prefer to journal. What works for you is fine. My only request is that you give it uninterrupted time.

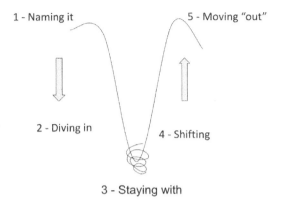

1 - Naming it - When you connect with the impact of the pandemic what is present for you? What is your pain, your bruise?

Can you give it a name?

A metaphor?

An image?

2 - Dive in it - Examine, explore, feel, notice the impact of "it". This stage can be longer for some, give it space. Be brave, be creative, write, draw, talk, tears are ok, be with yourself fully. You have permission here. Some of us feel like this takes us very low, some less so, it's ok, where you are is fine. If it feels too low, ask for help.

Staying with the image that came up for you above, how big or deep is your bruise?

How is that impacting you?

How is that impacting your relationships?

Anything else?

3 - Staying with - This place requires patience, bravery, and truthfulness. Emotions might be strong. You might experience a sense of loss of direction. Be curious, hold it,

draw it out. In this low point, what is happening for you here?

How are you really feeling?

Try to name the exact emotion

What is acutely present?

What is the colour? The sensation?

4 - Eventually something shifts - Don't force it, notice, when a thought, a light, a glimpse shows you hope. Your perspective might shift, a 2% shift is a shift. Observe it. Allow it to be, be gentle and take your time.

What was so hard, still is, but it feels different, you have now experienced the resilience to look into and to hold the bruise. You are slowly forming an acceptance of what was here.

Notice the thoughts that are opening a way

What is your heart saying?

5 - Moving out - As you allow your curiosity and self care to explore this new perspective, you notice a light, a renewed energy.

How will you move on from this emotion?

What is ahead for you?

Practice self love here. Things shift as our awareness has increased, and we have processed it.

Well done you! Let's celebrate your braveness.

Remember that this process will vary hugely from one individual to another. Give it space, time and a lot of love. Also, know when being alone does not work for you, know when asking for help would make the difference, be brave and ask for help. When it's too hard, know that you are not alone, help is here, ask for it.

3. For us - Collectively

No one is untouched

I've worked with many clients during the pandemic, and, certainly, it has been a hugely challenging period for the vast majority. It has been one of the toughest times for humanity that I have experienced. I rapidly observed the terminology of war that started to emerge - with curfews, lockdowns, front line etc - even Queen Elizabeth II referred to a famous Second World War song in her speech at the start of the pandemic saying "we will meet again"[15]. I felt the anxiety of my community and of society as a whole, building up strong and firm. I have felt the struggles among the people that I've worked with, the sense that they have been trying to hold everything together, attempting to be positive, or at least functional, managing the change, the distance from loved ones in many cases, and often dealing with fear. The grieving all around me has been abundantly clear. There is a tiredness, a lack of renewal; as if spring will never come and we've been plunged into an unending winter.

When working through this with Gunal, a highly rational and successful man, the metaphor of a long, dark and wet tunnel came up. He could see himself "legging" through

---

[15] Queen Elizabeth II, Covid-19's speech on 6 April 2020

the tunnel, pushing the boats thanks to the power of his legs, through a long and narrow and dark water tunnel. Legging was a new word for me, and I discovered through this powerful metaphor, this old method of moving a boat through a canal tunnel or a narrow waterway, dating from the 18th century. The pandemic felt hugely heavy, eating up an immense amount of energy, and pulling into his resources and resilience. As months passed, and as we worked through this period together he gradually moved through and out of the tunnel.

(Above: Image from the National Waterways Museum)

That's the dark side of the equation. The flip side is the resilience of humanity. As we've progressed through one, then two, then three and more lockdowns, I've marvelled at the incredible strength of people. It's quite impressive how readily human beings are able to accept, adapt and evolve when faced with the most unappetising changes in their lives. We've all had to cope with a revolution in our existence, which has occurred with a rapidity that would have been unimaginable just months ago. Yet people have coped. To a great extent, people have accepted the situation, made the best of it, and soldiered on. I remember vividly and with emotion when on 26 March 2020, millions of UK residents applauded for the medical workers who were tackling the front line of the pandemic. It was 8pm, and we opened our front door, and the sound of clapping, of whistles, of pans clicking rose up in the London sky. The event, initially called "Clap for our Carers" and apparently initiated by Annemarie Plas as she was inspired by others doing the same abroad, resonated through the country. For weeks, it became a ritual and every Thursday night we would clap. It would bring us joy, hope and a real sense of community. We could see, hear others, our neighbours close and far, all alive, noisy, cheering with hope. It had a real heartwarming and uplifting impact, but also a strong emotional reminder that we were in this together. We were showing gratitude for those who were working so hard, taking chances on their lives to support the community in this unprecedented time. A true support to each other through the cheer.

(Above: Clap for Carers - Hold Still, Anne Marie Plas[16])

Nonetheless, the challenges that many have faced have been all too evident. The situation, the confinement, is taking energy away from people. It is inevitable that psychological states have declined, and that the frustration that has been brewing within many of us has bubbled over in some cases. Freedom is the natural state of human beings, indeed of all animals, and there has been some inescapable resentment directed towards

---

[16] Hold Still: A Portrait of our Nation in 2020, by The Duchess of Cambridge Patron of the National Portrait Gallery and Lemn Sissay MBE 2021 - *Clap for Carers - Hold Still, Anne Marie Plas.*

anyone and anything that has reduced this liberty, independence and basic humanity.

The conditions associated with the Covid-19 pandemic and the lockdowns have varied based on geographical location. For example, in the toughest measures imposed in Spain, children were not permitted to leave their homes for several weeks. This would be a difficult situation for all households, and must have been particularly troublesome for families living in restrictive dwellings. Imagine a family of 3 or 4 children in a social housing settlement, or young children confined to a council flat for weeks on end - this is a fertile breeding ground for mental health problems, for violence, for anxiety and many other troubles. As the pandemic unfolded, the issues simply piled up; home working and homeschooling, cramped living quarters, diminution of freedom, schools closed, financial anxiety, agoraphobia - the problems just go on and on. In my own, relatively straightforward and lucky household, I know things did not feel easy or straightforward - I remember my 11 year old son lying on the floor at 11am on a Tuesday, with no willingness to get up, or stand, no sense of direction, and no appetite for another day inside. As I observed his body, expressing what most of us adults felt, in our minds and in our hearts, I connected with how strong children are at living and experiencing their feelings. I felt a real longing, a drag, a sadness, a loss of direction, a fear of getting up... it was all there.

The social and emotional impact of this situation cannot be overstated. We've been denied social contact, forced to stand metres apart from one another, required to refrain from hugging, reduced to a state of anxiety over financial issues (and some people have been absolutely ruined by the Covid-19 lockdown), separated irrevocably from our communities, denied access to our most nourishing hobbies and activities; even TV programmes and sport have been massively affected! The collective impact on ourselves, our communities, and our lives can only reasonably be described as bruising. We are all bruised right now. Even those of us that have lived in relatively fortunate circumstances during Covid, who may feel in a decent frame of mind, will still have some form of bruising.

I invite you to take a few moments to observe the impact of the pandemic around you

What was the impact of the pandemic on your community?

Who was most affected?

In the midst of this difficult time, did you notice any positive outcomes?

What is your impact on this community?

So that's where we are right now. And although conditions surrounding the pandemic might have eased, as I write these lines, the overall picture is still one of suffering and struggle. We can't just turn society back on again, and expect everyone to function as they did before. There has been a huge amount of collateral damage caused by the pandemic, and we are only now coming to terms with the reality and consequences of this.

For example, the Mental Health Foundation has collated data on the general population throughout the pandemic. And, naturally enough, as light has begun to appear at the end of this particularly prolonged tunnel, and society has begun to function in something approaching a customary fashion, mental health figures have generally become more encouraging. People began to feel hope, positivity and optimism once more.

However, what is also interesting and illustrative is the fact that some indicators of mental health continued to decline, even as society began to emerge from the gloomy depths of this crisis. Fewer people were worried about the virus, with levels of anxiety having noticeably declined from the beginning of the pandemic. But more people were lonely - rising from 10% in March 2020 to 26% in February 2021 - and feelings of hopelessness had particularly escalated in young people, with more than one-third (35%) reporting such emotions in February 2021[17].

It is not merely the virus and lockdowns themselves that have had an impact, but also the wider consequences. This has been particularly severe for young adults, many

---

[17] Mental Health Foundation. (2021). *Wave 10: Late February 2021: Emotional and mental wellbeing showing signs of recovery in some areas but not for all.*

of whom feel that some of the most important experiences of their lives have been cruelly snatched away from them, and also that their future prospects have been severely diminished. Indeed, the Office for National Statistics had already concluded by June 2020 that young adults would be hit hardest financially by Covid[18].

Statistics can succinctly illustrate the problems that people have faced, but often a picture communicates a thousand words. The National Portrait Gallery has produced a beautiful book "Hold Still"[19], spearheaded by The Duchess of Cambridge - described as a *"community project to create a unique collective portrait of the UK during the lockdown. They invited people of all ages to submit portraits taken between May and June 2020, focussed on three core themes – Helpers and Heroes, Your New Normal and Acts of Kindness"*. The 100 portraits chosen are emblematic of the suffering, the grief, the calamity of the Covid-19 situation. I've selected 2 to illustrate my point here, but I'll let you connect with this beautiful book of collective art and find your own wisdom there.

The first image, "The Long Awaited Cuddle" by Lesley Garven, is particularly powerful to me as it represents the

---

[18] Office for National Statistics. (2020). *More than one-fifth of usual household spending has been largely prevented during lockdown.*
[19] National Portrait Gallery. (2020). *Hold Still.*

lack of physical contact and its impact. I see in the intensity of this cuddle our human need for contact, and love.

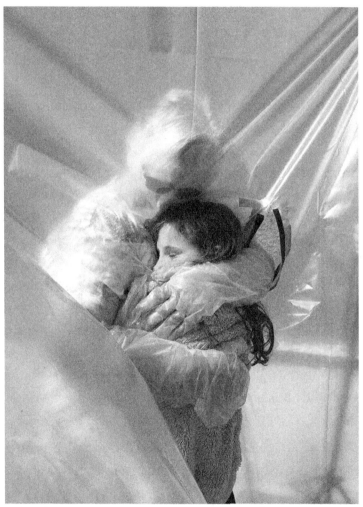

"The Long Awaited Cuddle"[20]

---

[20] Hold Still - National Portrait Gallery. (2020). *Long-Awaited Cuddle.*

The second image I've chosen is "This is What Broken Looks Like" by Ceri Hayles. As I observe this beautiful woman, I find that the bruise is visible, the eyes, the gaze, the skin, say a lot more than words could. The bruise is inside and out. On top of honouring the courage and resilience of medical and care staff it shows the pain, and the suffering the pandemic has created for many of us.

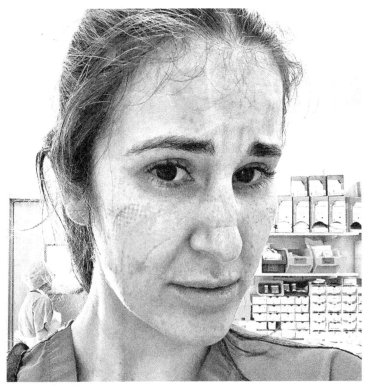

"This is What Broken Looks Like"[21]

---

[21]Hold Still - National Portrait Gallery. (2020). *This is What Broken Looks Like.*

In summary, there has never been a time in the last 70 years - dating back to the Second World War and immediate post-war period - where the general population, on an almost spectrum-wide basis, has endured such an episode of mental, emotional and psychological bruising. The collective consequences of this are massive. People have suffered and also showed up with strength and resilience. We will not emerge from this scenario unscathed, but we can and will come through it, beginning by increasing our awareness of the consequences of the pandemic. Let's acknowledge this for us as individuals as well as in our communities.

Edges

Acknowledging the situation has also been difficult because it is a situation that has been thrust upon us; few people anticipated or predicted that something of this nature would occur. I know that a few great minds, such as Bill Gates in 2015[22], had predicted the risk of a global pandemic, but in reality in November 2019 the world did not anticipate or expect the impact of Covid to be what it has become. We were not ready.

It takes being brave and self-reflective to understand the extent of what we've been through. I encourage doing it so that when we do heal, when we do bounce back and reconnect with our true reserves of energy, we do it in the right way, with purpose and giving it time and space. From a coaching perspective, the image and analogy that I would use is that we cross an edge, or a fence.

And when we cross an edge, we move from what is a known reality on one side, to the unknown on the other side of the divide. When you're in the known space, you know what to expect, you're in familiar turf, your surroundings are customary and comfortable, and you feel a sense of security about the situation. As change happens, we cross into the unknown.

---

[22] TED Talks. (2015). *Bill Gates - The next outbreak - We are not ready.*

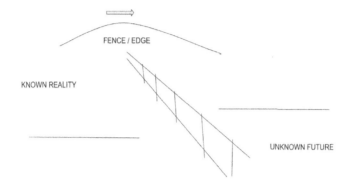

I want to bring the focus on this moment when change happens, when we are sitting on this fence, on the edge of it, and feel - on edge. On this edge we observe behaviours or emotions associated with the 3 Fs - Flight, Fight or Freeze. Drawing from the work at the start of the last century of the American physiologist, Walter Cannon[23], many current psychologists have refined and developed our understanding of how we react to threat and acute change. Drawing from these learnings and from my own work, I've observed some clients reacting with an acute sense of fear, some with nervous laughter, while others respond with anger and aggression. I find this space when change is about to happen, when we are not quite sure what will happen next and when nothing feels

---

[23] Cannon, W. B. (1915). *Bodily changes in pain, hunger, fear and rage: An account of recent researches into the function of emotional excitement.* D Appleton & Company.

certain which is a perfect breeding ground for negative behaviours and feelings.

Now, I invite you to take a step back and acknowledge the amount of uncertainty and change you have been through, as an individual, but also as a family member, as a worker, or business owner. Change and uncertainty have been everywhere, and a constant since the pandemic started. We've been on this fence, on edge for a long while now, and my impression is that we've been on the edge multiple times during the pandemic. Not only as individuals, but also as communities. And as we pan further out, regions, nations, continents, the entire planet has been in this zone, in this position of being on the edge. Even today, we still find ourselves sitting on the fence, not quite knowing what the future holds.

And that's not a comfortable place to be.

(Photo by Hasnain Babar on Unsplash)

The image that keeps coming to mind throughout this whole situation is that of a big field. Almost something reminiscent of childhood. A huge, open expanse that goes on well into the distance, over the horizon and beyond. We'd love to roam out into the middle of it, so that we can enjoy the feeling of the grass under our feet and be close to nature. But right now it's flooded. There's an enormous pool of water submerging the entire area, forcing us to fall back. And so we've been compelled to retreat to a wooden fence, which runs around the perimeter of this verdant pasture. And we're just sitting there. We're stuck. We've all had to run off together and take refuge on this wooden construction.

Sitting on a fence for a few minutes is acceptable, but it's not a long-term strategy, it's not comfortable. It gets pretty awkward, pretty quickly. We can't quite assume a natural posture. There are splinters. This is exactly the situation we've been in with the lockdown. We've been perched precariously in this abnormal and unaccustomed situation for much longer than any of us could have imagined. And then there is an extra layer of tension spooned on top of that. We are perhaps afraid of one another. We're scared to be around each other. So what could be an idyllic situation, rambling in the countryside, instead induces anxiety and gnawing discomfort. We get cramps, we become bruised, we have to unpick the splinters from our skin. And that's where we've been sitting, around the world, through various levels of home confinements or lockdowns.

The reality is that we've all been in this situation for longer than is healthy. Even the authorities have acknowledged this. And now it's time to slowly ease ourselves off the fence, bringing our feet back to earth once more. This should be the most natural thing in the world, yet returning back to a form of normality doesn't seem quite as green and pleasant as it once was. And there is some nagging uncertainty hanging in the air. How will we go back to work? Can we travel freely? What will the new reality look like? Is it possible to return to our old routines and practices? Can we really completely leave the fence, or are we still somewhat in limbo?

This is the ironic thing; we've all wanted this for so long, but now that we're confronted with the prospect of freedom, it's slightly unsettling. We're collectively like a vintage car that has been stored in a garage for years, and now the engine doesn't hum with the vigour that it should. There are a lot of unanswered questions about this new reality that is now beginning to unfold. And a lot of us have yet to even address the bruises and scars that we've accumulated, let alone heal them.

We cannot heal if we're not willing to acknowledge the unprecedented change and disruption that we've all been through. Change brings uncertainty, change brings a lot of mixed emotions, and change can lead to a negative mental state, particularly when the change is undesirable. And some people are simply better equipped to deal with this change than others. That's okay. We're all different.

An English psychologist, John Fischer has drawn a model "The Personal Transition Curve[24]" which I find helpful and

---

[24]John Fischer - https://www.r10.global/wp-content/uploads/2017/05/fisher-transition-curve-2012-1.pdf

pertinent if we apply it to the changes we have been through. It shows and normalises how individuals deal and feel through change. We might feel connected with some of the stages more strongly than others, but having experienced it myself, and worked through this with hundreds of clients, I find most people will recognise themselves and their emotions on this graph.

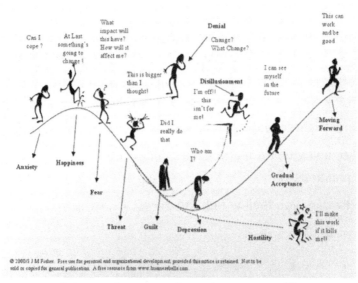

(Above: Change Toolkit - Change Curve[25])

---

[25]John Fischer's Change Curve - http://www.changetoolkit.org.uk/change-curve/

Time to reflect

So I'd like you, as a reader, to think what is here for you right now?

I invite you to look deep inside yourself and acknowledge the scars that the pandemic has created, to neither judge nor deny it, or even pretend that it's something different to what it is. Just accept it. There is no right or wrong here. And it can be something that comes in stages, or via creative activities. I encourage drawing, painting, singing, music, whatever feels right to go with the emotions that you feel. See where the emotion takes you because this often manifests itself in creativity, energy and movement. Be ready to go there, to explore that emotion, and investigate what it is telling you.

So, being truthful and vulnerable, consider the following questions:

How are you feeling right now?

Reflecting back on how you have evolved since the start of the pandemic, how have you been doing?

Draw a timeline of your emotions using the curve below. Take a pencil and draw your emotional state against time, going above and under the middle line according to how you felt. Reconnect with the events in the outside world, and notice the impact they may have had on you.

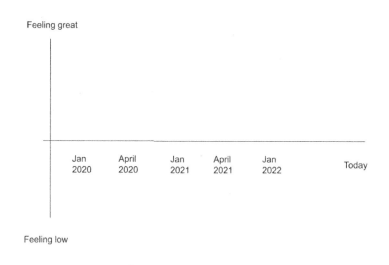

Feeling great

| Jan 2020 | April 2020 | Jan 2021 | April 2021 | Jan 2022 | Today |

Feeling low

Looking at your "feeling line"-

What were the lows? When did they happen? What was happening in your life?

1st low -

2nd low -

3rd low -

Other

What were the highs? When did they happen? What was happening in your life?

1st high -

2nd high -

3rd high -

Other

How would you describe the impact of the pandemic on you?

How did you cope?

Considering the impact of the pandemic, and using the image of the bruise, what does this bruise look like? Can you draw it?

How deep, or shallow is it?

What colour is it?

Is it painful? Infected or just superficial?

How long do you think it will take to heal?

Will it leave any scars?

How can you clean it, and take care of it?

Today, how does it feel?

We can heal if we allow space and time. If we open ourselves to what is here, to our feelings and give our bruised bodies love, we will heal.

We've all been impacted by the Covid-19 pandemic. The cumulative effect of the absence of positive experiences, intense and recurrent stressful news, restraint of freedom, fear for our health and that of others and the lack of social contact have a major psychological and well-being impact.

We will not emerge from this scenario unscathed, but we can come through it, beginning by increasing our awareness of the personal consequences of the pandemic. Processing this impact involves working with our emotions and identifying our present state. Awareness and, particularly, self-awareness are critical components of this process.

Part II
And Pause …

It serves us well to slow down and focus on what is here, just lurking beneath the surface, which we might ignore otherwise. In this part of the book, I focus on the importance of taking a pause and slowing down. Like a breathing space in between 2 races. Let's recharge, take some time to practice self-care and to refill the energy and happiness tank.

The key here is not to rush. Sometimes we just need to stop and pause. Rest, recalibrate and recognise. And then we can move forward.

So now that we've acknowledged the collective pain, I think it's important for us to examine our own wounds. Looking at how they feel for you as an individual, and maybe also the wounds that your loved ones and family have incurred. What I emphasise with my clients is that change is a steady process. It's not rapid, it's not hurried, it's one step at a time. It's natural to want to heal quickly, however when you feel a bruise, be ready to take your time in addressing it.

The process also requires bravery, as it takes courage to examine what is painful, just like a physical wound. Many people get through life by shutting off their deep feelings, and repressing anything too painful, or even anaesthetising the pain with alcohol, drugs, or by overdoing it. But this is no sort of solution - life passes you by.

This takes time, and requires what I call 'brain space' to examine your reality. If I look at what is here in the present for myself, it has definitely evolved throughout the pandemic. I initially felt this collective weight on my shoulders. Even just connecting with it right now makes so much emotion surface again. It was pretty heavy! Sadness, pain, the sense of loss that was almost tangible in the air... I can feel them all again. At the time, I could feel it in my bones, in my heart, it became part of me. In this section I invite you to take a step back, to reflect on the balance in your life - not just the "work / life" balance, a full holistic view on the important things in your life. As we launch this reflection I'll invite you to slow right down, to lower the pace, to lower the volume, and distractions around you - just for a little while. Practice self-care, reconnect with yourself, with your loved ones and gradually reconnect back to the world around you.

4. Balcony view

Your wheel of life

I encountered a huge amount of examples from my coaching work of people that struggle to take a step back, to connect with what is important to them and invest in the self-care and self-love that they need. For example, Kumar wanted to change career, in a radically different direction. So when we started working together, the discussion began on a fairly practical level, discussing the potential for a career change, and how this would progress. When I'm working with a client, I work with the whole person, as I find this is the most truthful and empowering approach to the process. We work with everything that you are as an individual, so that we can understand you in a holistic fashion. Naturally, one's career is important, but how you make career choices, why you make career choices, and your underlying motivations that ensure your next move correlates with your internal purpose, is absolutely essential. It paves the way to be your authentic self, and to connect with your raison d'être.

On one occasion, as I was working with Kumar, and we were opening up this place of purpose, of life purpose, that would be sustaining and fulfilling for him going forward. But there was so much resistance to explore what was deeper inside, as he felt a very real fear of the pain that he had experienced in the recent past. Essentially, he had lost his role in life. It was a gentleman who had been made redundant from a top investment bank. He felt like a failure. He had achieved a lot, but the fact that he hadn't been able to climb and climb and climb, reaching higher and higher in his career, was a defeat from his perspective, almost an embarrassment. He had stalled and fallen, and he viewed this as a fundamental failing. And when he spoke to me, it was the first time that he had actually addressed this profound sense of grief and loss; the feelings that had undermined him when he was made redundant. This fear that he had been holding inside himself for the last 4 years had prevented him from moving forward in life, from being brave and making the career choices that would be the best approach, and that would set him on the path to fulfilment and happiness. Thankfully, we were able to work together closely, to acknowledge and examine this internal suffering, and the process helped him to let go, to address the situation, and to make the commitment to move forward. It was a wonderful coaching experience for me, and an important moment in his life.

This is why I often start a new coaching relationship by encouraging my clients to reflect on their overall satisfaction in life. The aim is to lift the head up from the thoughts and troubles of the day to day and to take this balcony view on their life - the magic of perspective.

We acknowledge that the overall satisfaction in life might change from one day to another, and that's absolutely normal. What we aim to narrow down are the areas where there is balance, satisfaction and a sense of fulfilment and the other side, the areas where there might be scope to work on and to progress.

The 8 sections represent different aspects of your life which contribute to your overall fulfilment.

I invite you to rank your level of satisfaction (out of 10) in each area by drawing a line and tracing the perimeter of your life. 10 represents full satisfaction.

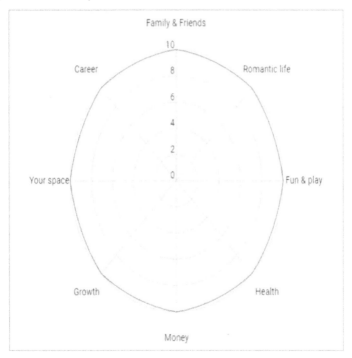

Notice the overall shape. Is it spiky? Is it round? Is it narrow or wide?

What are you noticing about your overall satisfaction in life?

Now select a few of the lower scores, and reflect or journal your answers to the questions below.

Select one of the dimensions and for this topic journal your answers to the following questions:

- What gives this topic such a low score?

- In the reality that you are in, what would make it an 8 or 9?

- What do you have an impact on? What could you do differently to achieve this?

- What would make it a 10?

Select another dimension - as above, journal your answers to the following questions:

- What gives this topic such a low score?

- In the reality that you are in, what would make it an 8 or 9?

- What do you have an impact on? What could you do differently to achieve this?

- What would make it a 10?

Select another dimension - again, journal your answers to the following questions:

- What gives this topic such a low score?

- In the reality that you are in, what would make it an 8 or 9?

- What do you have an impact on? What could you do differently to achieve this?

- What would make it a 10?

Keep going, and apply the same questions to all the dimensions if necessary.

Now that you've taken a step back on the overall satisfaction in your life, what are you learning about your current situation?

Are there any actions that would help you increase this satisfaction?

Out of balance?

Another helpful approach to help reflection on your overall well being is to draw your attention to your inner balance. As a coach, one of the dichotomies that I work with on a regular basis is the concept of "Being" versus "Doing". This is one of the most important balances in life. I often liken it to a seesaw, similar to the one that I used to play on in kindergarten. One of the simplest and most traditional toys, yet still popular with young people. Basically just a plank of wood, with children sitting on either end, going up and down, up and down continually.

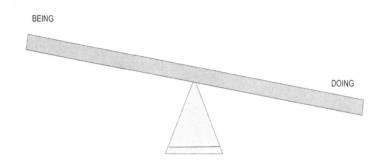

BEING

DOING

The seesaw is a wonderful analogy for life in many ways, but particularly for this ongoing balance between "Being" and "Doing". On one side of the seesaw is the Being. This is the ability to be present with our emotions and thoughts, to be aware of what is happening right now, at a particular frozen moment in time. Part of this process is allowing the emotions, the thoughts, the things inside ourselves to which we don't always pay attention to come out. Being is a receptive and contemplative state, and it's an important part of life.

On the other end of the seesaw is the Doing part of life. And I'm sure that many people reading this book will relate to this. It's certainly a place where my life and world tends to be focused. I feel that our culture and society hugely values 'doers'. The more that you do, the more that you achieve, the greater your ability to multitask, the more that you are treasured and put on a pedestal. It almost becomes one unending cycle of having multiple projects on the go, constantly keeping them moving, and attempting to achieve more and more with less and less time. You become like the magician spinning plates, trying to keep them all from falling and shattering on the floor.

This ability of doing is particularly valued in the professional world. I encounter a huge number of clients who are brilliant doers, who are constantly getting stuff done, and have no end of projects and ambitions, which they attack with seemingly boundless energy. This mentality of being driven and task-oriented can often lead to a very dynamic and fast-paced lifestyle. It's the outlook that makes the world go round, and generally one that is essential for anyone going into business.

When we consider these two states of being and doing, they are fundamentally different expressions of being human. One is very reflective and inward-looking, while the other is focused on activity and external achievements. So if we come back to the seesaw, the ideal scenario would be for these two to be in an equilibrium. For the two weights at either end of the seesaw to be calibrated to allow 'balance'. We can tilt the seesaw one way, but then it can just as easily return to the opposite position; just as a seesaw is designed to operate.

Of course, that's not always the case. And this doesn't just differ from one person to another, the balance between these two states can definitely fluctuate in every single one of us, as our lives change and evolve.

To take the former first, if the being end of the seesaw is too elevated and out of balance, this is when you're prone to procrastination. You become so profoundly preoccupied with your thoughts and feelings that you are almost paralysed. You fail to do anything, and you are unable to progress in your own life, as you're too focused on the introspective concerns that you have about your own thoughts, ideas, feelings and state of being.

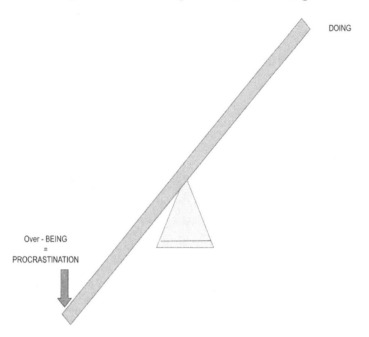

Then the contrasting state would be one of extreme doing. When you're taking on far too much responsibility, engaging in an excessive amount of activity, and simply driving yourself far too hard. Again, this usually happens because you fail to listen to your body adequately, thus you are unable to heed your thoughts and emotions; some of your key indicators as a human being. At this point, you run the risk of burning yourself out and completely shutting down. The body will literally force you into the opposite state, where you are inactive and resting, so that you can return to a state of balance.

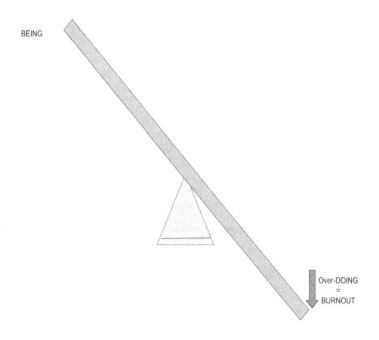

BEING

Over-DOING
=
BURNOUT

Neither of these extreme states are exactly desirable, but it's also important to understand that there is no right and wrong behaviour. There is certainly healthy and unhealthy behaviour, but we're not judging someone by saying that they're being too inactive, or indeed active. It's simply about understanding yourself and acknowledging where you are on the seesaw. As I mentioned previously, this not only differs from one person to another, it changes significantly during different times in our lives.

At no time has this been more true than during the recent lockdowns and pandemic. This had a profound influence over virtually everyone, and continues to do so. The whole concept of having the seesaw in balance has been completely jettisoned in many cases. Suddenly, the usual balance that we should seek in our lives has gone out of the window, simply due to logistical reasons.

So now we're picking ourselves up after one of the most disruptive times that we will ever encounter - although I should emphasise that the situation is certainly not over. And the consequences have been different for different people. Some of us might have had a lonely experience during the lockdown, descending into something of a slower mindset. This will almost inevitably see people sink into their emotions and thoughts, and in some cases they will actually struggle to move. It can be a difficult place to escape from if you become bogged down in this mindset.

On the flip side, other people during the pandemic probably found themselves with so much work to do and so many things to juggle, that they haven't had time to reflect on their emotions and thoughts. I know from my perspective, my family life has been hectic, I've been working on my coaching career, I had to take care of the house, while being a wife, a mother, a friend, a sister, and a daughter. And then, on top of that, I'm part of a French family, so food and mealtimes are important to us. That means that I'm cooking 15 meals every day. There was so much on my plate; so much that needed doing, and not enough hours in the day to get it done.

Much of the commentary on the research focused on the opportunity that the Covid-19 pandemic presents to reassess the way that we live our lives, as well as the demands that companies place on workers. "The Covid-19 pandemic has significantly changed the way many people work. Teleworking has become the norm in many industries, often blurring the boundaries between home and work. In addition, many businesses have been forced to scale back or shut down operations to save money, and people who are still on the payroll end up working longer hours. No job is worth the risk of stroke or heart disease. Governments, employers and workers need to work together to agree on limits to protect the health of workers,"[26] Dr Ghebreyesus commented.

Figures related to the pandemic years have yet to be analysed, but what is clear is that we all need to more carefully consider the way that we balance our working and recuperative lives, or indeed whether we have a recuperative life at all!

---

[26] Dr Tedros Adhanom Ghebreyesus, WHO Director-General,

Self-coaching exercise

So now is the time to acknowledge precisely where you are on the seesaw. It's possible that some people will have managed to retain a perfect balance throughout the pandemic. But many of us will have tilted precariously in one direction or another, and now we need to understand precisely where we are.

What was your balance during the pandemic?

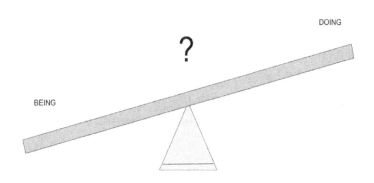

Did your balance shift?

What did you notice?

What sits on the being side?

What sits on the doing side?

Where are you today?

Do you need to re-balance? If so, what would help you rebalance?

Rather than addressing a shift immediately, my recommendation is instead to simply pause. Just pause, just observe and just be with whatever is here. Just notice for yourself, until you recognise your position and state. Ask yourself what you need to do, or stop doing, if you are to readjust, so that you manage to restore the balance in your own life. And then when you return to this position of being in equilibrium, things will start to unfold, and your life will begin to get better. Your emotional state will improve.

I know for myself that I have a tendency to settle on the doing side of the device. This doesn't just apply to the pandemic; it is part of my makeup as a human being. For example, I used to work as a lawyer before moving into my current profession, and I remember taking the bar exam, the final part of my law degree course, precisely two weeks after giving birth to my firstborn baby. And I also remember feeling proud of that achievement, believing it to be a huge accomplishment. But with the wisdom of hindsight, I'm not sure that I should be so proud of this. I think that I was overdoing it with exams and studies, and I failed to get the balance right at that time. Naturally, when you become a mother for the first time, you want to cherish being with your baby. You want to be fully present in the moment, and reflecting on this joyous occasion. Sometimes you can choose, sometimes it's harder, but I find recognising I may have "Done" too much helps me accept it and "Be" with what is now important.

If I had the chance to go back and reassess this period of my existence, I would definitely try to rebalance my priorities. I would Be more and Do less. I believe many, many people are now in this precise situation of needing to assess their current position. There has been this period of incredible change, of grief for many of us, and now is the time to reassess our priorities. What is your balance like currently? What do you need in order to realign it? How will you get back into a position of being in balance? These are some of the key questions that millions of people need to consider and address.

Additionally, it's not just acknowledging the impact of the pandemic on the individual. I think we also need to assess what the effect has been on us collectively, on a community and societal level. And in order to do this, many of us will need to slow down, so that we can just be in a natural state with our feelings, our emotions, the pain, the joy, the sometimes beautiful, sometimes agonising side of our existence. And we need to do this so that we can move forward in a healthy and more balanced fashion.

The danger of overdoing is to burn ourselves out, and that can be dangerous. What we need to do is stop, pause and reflect. As you are inviting this self reflection, allow space and time. Give yourself permission to pause, to reflect so that when the time is right, you can bounce back in a mindful and purposeful way.

5. Self-Compassion

Super-Powers

I want to acknowledge that it can be difficult to look inside ourselves. Even the most formidable and successful people can find it almost impossible to acknowledge the grief and pain that they have experienced. We have physiological and psychological processes that attempt to stop us from examining things like this; it's a natural defence or self-protection mechanism against feeling pain and suffering. However, I've noticed that if we don't examine our pain, if we're not willing to put it under the microscope, it does not heal.

I view this place of having the courage to peer inside yourself as being an act of self respect. This is an act of self-love; a practice of valuing yourself, your body, your mind, and your life in order to give yourself what you deserve. Sometimes loving ourselves, or even just accepting ourselves, can be hard. Often we carry a huge amount of opinions or judgement with us, and they prevent us from giving ourselves the self-love that we deserve. If only we were able to do it, life would become so much lighter and more joyful, with happiness and fulfilment often following quickly behind. I often tell my children - happiness is not something that just lands on you. It's a journey. You have to work at it.

Take a few moments to capture your strengths. To reconnect with what you are good at, and what you enjoy doing. To fill up our energy tank, we must nurture our self-love and remind ourselves what we are good at, and the positive impact we have on the world around us. This is not a boastful practice, it's a vulnerable, truthful and heartful exercise, of being truly transparent with yourself, of quieting the voice who might be telling you "you are not good enough, or not worth it, or not strong enough". You are leaning into your wise self and on what you are proud of. Let's reflect:

What are you proud of?

What do people enjoy about you?

Do not judge or diminish what is coming up - let it rise to the surface, breathe deeply into this acknowledgement of yourself. You are a wonderful human being.

Recollect last time you received some praise - what positive things did people say about you?

What are your key strengths?

What makes you different from others, and how does this make you feel strong?

Positive mindset

Earlier in the book, we mentioned the importance of positive psychology, and how this has become a significant force within both psychology as an academic subject and the practice of psychology, and the implementation of psychological treatments in the real world. One of the interesting aspects of this school of psychology is the concept of positive affirmation; quite simply, the practice of using positive phrases and / or statements to challenge negative thoughts, and help create new, more constructive thought patterns.

This might appear a little woolly at first, but there is actually strong scientific evidence backing up the notion that positive affirmations can produce positive emotions and outcomes. Indeed, there is an entire body of academic theory already backing up this concept, which was recognised and labelled as 'self-affirmation' theory as early as 1988.[27] There are actually a multitude of studies that suggest we can maintain our sense of self-integrity simply by telling ourselves what we believe in a positive manner.

Before we go into the specifics of self-affirmation in more detail, it's first interesting to consider why this practice actually works! The key factor here is the neuroplasticity of the brain - which means its ability to adapt to different

---

[27]https://www.sciencedirect.com/science/article/abs/pii/S0065260108602294

circumstances. Your brain has evolved to evolve! It will change as it encounters different environments and inputs, and, actually, our own thoughts form an important part of this process. We change our thinking by the way that we think – truly a chicken and egg situation!

Nonetheless, we can take advantage of this situation. Our brains struggle to differentiate between reality and imagination, hence the fact that our own thoughts can feed our brain chemistry to such a significant degree. If we're constantly nourishing our brain with negative affirmations, such as "I am not good enough", we are bombarding ourselves with thousands of mini-traumas. So the way that we use language when we're dealing with our own self-image is important. It's critically important. Arguably, it has as much of an impact on our sense of self as external events and genetics. We create our own mental image of ourselves, and often this can be completely different from how we are perceived by others. In fact, I would argue that most people's self-image is far removed from how they are seen in the eyes of their family, friends, colleagues, and peers.

What this means is that most of us have some work to do in crafting a self-image that is genuinely supportive of being the best version of ourselves. And positive affirmation is an effective way of at least beginning the journey towards achieving this. Because it's known, for example, that creating an affirmative mental image of yourself achieving something activates many of the same brain areas as actually doing it; hence why visualisation is such a widely advocated technique, particularly in sports psychology. When you truly believe you can do something and you've already pictured this happening in your mind, often you can do it, even when the activity in question is immensely difficult or you're pitted against stiff competition.

There are 3 key concepts that underpin self-affirmation theory. The first is that by utilising self-affirmation we are creating a global narrative that effectively creates our self-identity. This notion was discussed extensively in a 2014 study authored by Cohen and Sherman:

"Self-affirmation interventions bring about a more expansive view of the self and its resources, weakening the implications of a threat for personal integrity. Timely affirmations have been shown to improve education, health, and relationship outcomes, with benefits that sometimes persist for months and years.[28]"

This means that we can be flexible, enabling us to adapt to a variety of different situations.

Secondly, self-affirmation theory asserts that you don't have to be perfect to maintain your self-identity, but rather adequate in areas that we particularly value. And, finally, we maintain self-integrity by acting in ways that

---

[28] The Psychology of Change: Self-Affirmation and Social Psychological Intervention - Jan 2014 Annual Review of Psychology 65(1):333-71

authentically merit acknowledgment and praise. We don't praise ourselves simply because we wish to receive praise, we do it because we've behaved in a manner that is consistent with our values, and that is therefore worthy of praise. This is vital to achieve the authenticity required for self-affirmation to reap positive rewards.

Speaking of values, one of the most useful processes that we can undertake before engaging in self-affirmation is to establish our core values. These are our guiding principles; the qualities we value most that are the fundamental building blocks of our character. These core values differ from one person to another, but establishing and being aware of them is a critically important pillar of self-knowledge.

And if we don't know ourselves then achieving any lasting happiness or fulfilment will be challenging, as when we are presented with forks in the road we are essentially stabbing in the dark. We don't know which way to turn because we don't know ourselves, and therefore we don't know what will make us happy. Whereas once we have this foundation of self-knowledge provided by an awareness of our core values, this can then inform all of our key decisions.

It's important to delineate your core values at the outset, as research has demonstrated that self-affirmations must reflect your core values in order to be truly effective.[29] You may gain some benefit from repeating more generic statements, but the practice won't achieve its maximum potential unless your affirmations are aligned with your authentic self. In order to achieve an impact on your self-esteem, self-affirmations should be, not only positively focused, but targeted at areas that reinforce your sense of self-identity. You don't use self-affirmation to change who you are; you use the technique to celebrate who you are already.

The science underlying self-affirmation is actually quite well-established. A study published in the journal Social Cognitive and Affective Neuroscience demonstrated via MRI scanning that self-affirmation activates the reward centre of your brain, which is associated with pleasurable and joyful activities. By making the most basic affirmative statements, your neural pathways will essentially light up, making constructive changes to the areas of the brain that make you feel happy and positive about life.

Self-affirmation is an interesting example of the cognitive biases that exist within all of us. While our brains are capable of deep thinking they are also designed to make snap decisions for reasons of survival. There isn't always time to calculate all of the possibilities in a developing situation; sometimes we are forced to make a snap

---

[29] https://www.annualreviews.org/doi/abs/10.1146/annurev-psych-010213-115137

decision, or perish! As a result of this, the brain continually creates shortcuts so that we can make those quick judgements that are sometimes needed in life.

Consequently, self-affirmation works well. Specifically, the ventromedial prefrontal cortex - involved in positive valuation and self-related information processing - becomes more active when we consider our personal values. The study from 2015 that confirmed this via MRI scanning asserted that those who practice positive affirmations will be better able to view "otherwise-threatening information as more self-relevant and valuable".[30]

And there is a lot of other academic research that also corroborates the value of self-affirmation, demonstrating that the practice can have a range of psychological and physical benefits. Here is the background to some of the published studies on this subject:

- Stress - A study published in the Health Psychology journal in 2009 found that self-affirmation can help decrease health-deteriorating stress. The authors concluded that "the findings demonstrate that sympathetic nervous system responses to naturalistic stressors can be attenuated by self-affirmation. Discussion centres on psychological pathways by which affirmation can reduce stress and the implications

---

[30] https://www.pnas.org/content/112/7/1977

of the findings for health outcomes among chronically stressed participants."[31]

- Physical activity - Research published in The Journal of Sport & Exercise Psychology in 2014, involving a longitudinal study of 80 young people, discovered that self-affirmations can be used effectively in interventions that led to people becoming more physically active. "Self-affirmation interventions have the potential to become relatively simple methods for increasing physical activity levels," the study concluded.[32]

- Health interventions - An influential study from 2012 demonstrated that health interventions that would otherwise be threatening or difficult to comply with can be more readily promoted when self-affirmation is implemented. The work of Logel and Cohen with a group of women attempting to achieve weight loss found that "women who completed a values affirmation weighed less, had lower BMIs, and had smaller waistlines than women who had not completed a values affirmation when the two groups were examined after a 2.5-month interval."[33] Similarly,

[31] https://psycnet.apa.org/record/2009-14439-006

[32] https://pubmed.ncbi.nlm.nih.gov/24686957/

[33] https://www.researchgate.net/publication/51867629_The_Role_of_the_Self_in_Physical_Health_Testing_the_Effect_of_a_Values-Affirmation_Intervention_on_Weight_Loss

in a 2007 study, smokers were less defensive about anti-smoking messages on cigarette packets after sustained self-affirmation.[34]

- Academic achievement - Self-affirmation has also been linked to improved academic achievement, particularly in a 2017 study which found that "affirmation intervention mitigated - and even reversed - the decline in GPA among students with a low sense of belonging in college, providing support for self-affirmation theory's contention that affirmations of personal integrity can lessen psychological threat regardless of its source."[35]

These are just some examples of academic literature on the potential benefits of self-affirmation. In general terms, affirmations encourage an optimistic mindset, which then enables us to construct more adaptive and hopeful narratives about ourselves and our potential accomplishments.

Positive affirmations should be personal to you, but it's still possible to give some examples of the sort of statements that can be constructive. Here are a few examples:

- I choose to be happy.

[34] https://psycnet.apa.org/record/2007-09406-007
[35] https://psycnet.apa.org/record/2016-49095-001

- I love myself, as I am - full of beauty and imperfections.

- I am grateful for my wonderful support network of friends and family.

- I am strong, brave and confident, and I will achieve my goals.

- Nobody but me decides how I feel.

- My goals and desires are worthwhile and important.

- My body is amazing and I accept myself the way that I am.

- I will only surround myself with good and positive people.

- Through courage and hard work, I can achieve anything.

Positive affirmation is just one aspect of an overall practice of mindfulness that can be useful. Again, it's not necessarily for everyone, but it can be highly useful, and it's important to understand that the benefits have been well-established, both in terms of scientific research and in everyday practice.

6. Slowing right down

Mindfulness and meditation

To build a practice of self compassion and self respect, you will find that incorporating a habit to reflect or a space to let your mind wander, will be incredibly resourceful. It changes lives - I've seen it many times.

Practices and concepts such as mindfulness and meditation have certainly become more vogueish in recent years. If you went back perhaps 30-40 years, certainly in Western society it would have been unusual to engage in any meditation practice, while the concept of mindfulness certainly wasn't part of common discourse. But today, we are fully aware of the potential benefits of these ideas and practices, which can only be a good thing, in my opinion.

> *"In the midst of movement and chaos, keep stillness inside you.[36]"*

Meditation and mindfulness both serve the purpose of taking a pause, looking deep inside ourselves as individuals, seeing what's there, observing and accepting this reality. In my perception, and as an attempt to define

---

[36]In The Midst Of Movement And Chaos Keep Stillness Inside Of You Deepak Chopra - 2020, Deepak Chopra

the 2, meditation is the focus of your mind, (such as the focus on nature, on music on a painting, on your feelings etc.) Mindfulness is a form of meditation, where you focus on being present with your body and your feelings or emotions. The aim is to accept what is here, to be curious and just to be with it.

I find we're often encouraged to be pursuing something, or striving to achieve a new goal. For some the pace of life has become so desperately frantic, it's not surprising that many people experience psychological difficulties and even breakdowns. Francesca, a senior partner in a top recruiting firm realised through our work that she was so taken by her work and endless responsibilities that it was affecting her breathing. She was holding her breath while typing, working or delivering a presentation. The tightness in her chest was a result of the tension of her day to day, and this affected the quality of her breathing. Common sense led us to understand that the lack of air, and quality of her breathing had a ripple effect on her overall health and well being, and in full circle productivity at work. Realising this was groundbreaking for her - it came from slowing down, observing how she was being in her body while trying to deliver all her world expected from her. As a result, she focused every day on her breathing, taking time out to just breathe, and to rebalance her body needs with the rest.

With this in mind, I frequently encourage my clients to take a pause. I invite them to be curious, open, to observe and accept what they discover and feel inside themselves. When we go through this process, we often close our eyes and let our minds quieten slowly. We explore an emotion, something that they're living with, where the deepest-rooted feelings dwell. We'll focus on our breathing and just connect with the feeling. We might examine a metaphor, or connect with an image that emerges in their consciousness. At this point, I often encounter tears, or beaming smiles of pure joy, and this is where my clients connect with the truest side of themselves.

The weight of academic research supporting these practices, and the scope of benefits associated with them, is quite astonishing. Here are just some the examples that have been established in recent years:

- Meditation helps keep your brain healthy - One study from UCLA found that those who meditated over a prolonged period of time enjoyed better brain preservation as they aged. Study author Florian Kurth noted that "what we actually observed was a widespread effect of meditation that encompassed regions throughout the entire brain."[37]

---

[37]http://journal.frontiersin.org/Journal/10.3389/fpsyg.2014.01551/full

- Mindfulness successfully treats depression - A study from Johns Hopkins University examined the relationship between mindfulness meditation and its ability to reduce symptoms of depression, anxiety, and pain. Researchers found that it was as effective as antidepressants. Researcher Madhav Goyal commented that "A lot of people have this idea that meditation means sitting down and doing nothing. But that's not true. Meditation is an active training of the mind to increase awareness, and different meditation programs approach this in different ways."[38]

- Meditation training rapidly improves concentration and attention - A recent study found that after merely two weeks of meditation training participants were able to achieve improved results in a verbal reasoning test. In fact, the increase in performance was the equivalent of 16%.[39]

- Meditation reduces anxiety, including social anxiety - There is strong evidence to support the notion that meditation reduces stress; indeed, there is an entire field of meditation referred to as Mindfulness-Based Stress Reduction (MBSR).

---

[38]https://jamanetwork.com/journals/jamainternalmedicine/fullarticle/1809754

[39]https://journals.sagepub.com/doi/abs/10.1177/0956797612459659

Mindfulness and meditation have repeatedly demonstrated their ability to reduce stress and anxiety, in a variety of testing settings[40].

- Meditation helps with addiction - Several studies have indicated that meditation can reduce the grip of various addictions. One of the most compelling, published in the Drug and Alcohol Dependency journal, used two groups to assess the American Lung Association's freedom from smoking program. Those who used mindfulness as part of their treatment were many times more likely to have quit smoking by the end of the training, and at 17 weeks follow-up, than those in the conventional treatment.[41]

These are just some of the many valuable physical and psychological benefits that have been discovered to result from the practice of meditation and mindfulness. Having said that, it's important to note that mindfulness and meditation don't work miracles for everyone. They're not necessarily something that I advocate as such, rather I will suggest to clients that these practices are something that could potentially be valuable, that slowing down and taking care is at the essence of these exercises.

---

[40] Zen meditation, Length of Telomeres, and the Role of Experiential Avoidance and Compassion
Marta Alda, Marta Puebla-Guedea, Baltasar Rodero, Marcelo Demarzo, Jesus Montero-Marin, Miquel Roca, and Javier Garcia-Campayo
[41] https://pubmed.ncbi.nlm.nih.gov/21723049/

My challenge to all readers is to look inside yourselves and ask honestly what it is that you're not willing to feel. What is it that you're holding back? What scares you? And if you're willing to go there and examine these questions, be ready to examine the bruise that emerges. Have a look at the pain, and see precisely what is there. It might be big, it might be small, but whatever size it might be is perfectly okay. You might have been deeply wounded and scarred by this pandemic, or it might be a small bruise that will go numb for a little while, and then go away. But sit with it, quietly contemplate it in a state of being, and acknowledge what is actually there.

This is what meditation is all about. It's the ability to just be, to exist in awareness of one's self, and to examine this state openly and honestly.

Emotional intelligence

I believe our ability to work on yourselves, to acknowledge that we need to slow down, to actually slow down, to maybe try practices such as mindfulness meditation or other forms to reflect is a sign of emotional intelligence. I've noticed people who do the work themselves are often highly emotionally intelligent. I will spend a few moments to elaborate what this means, and hopefully will give you an additional appetite to do the work for yourselves.

The notion of emotional intelligence which has been extensively researched and documented in the work of Daniel Goleman[42] - a Harvard Psychology professor. Goleman has demonstrated the power of developing emotional intelligence, as a tool to achieve and thrive in this world. His work drew heavily from the pioneers in this field, Peter Salovey and John Mayer, who originally developed the psychological theory of emotional intelligence. This was defined in a widely cited discussion from 1997, in which the two researchers established the following definition - as "*the ability to perceive emotions, integrate emotions to facilitate thought, understand emotions and to regulate emotions to promote personal growth.*" The following year, Goleman defined emotional intelligence as '*the capacity for recognizing our own*

---

[42] Emotional Intelligence: Why it matters more than IQ, 2020 Daniel Goleman

feelings and those of others, for motivating ourselves, and for managing emotions well in ourselves and in our relationships."[43] Goleman has since developed this theory considerably, having diligently researched the concept of emotional intelligence, writing a raft of well-received books on the subject. Central to this work has been Goleman's assertion that there are five components that collectively constitute emotional intelligence. These are as follows:

Self-awareness - this can be defined as the ability to recognise and understand personal moods, emotions and drives, as well as the impact that they have on other people. Realistic and ongoing self-assessment is central to this trait, as self-awareness is ultimately dependent on the ability to monitor one's state of mind and accurately identify your own emotions.

Self-regulation - this refers to the ability to respond to impulses, moods and emotional states, particularly with control and redirection. A key facet of this is to suspend judgement and to acknowledge what is here while keeping a form of control on your reactions. People with high levels of self-regulation tend to possess integrity, while being trustworthy and open to change.

[43] Mayer, J. D., & Salovey, P. (1997). What is emotional intelligence? In P. Salovey & D. J. Sluyter (Eds.), Emotional development and emotional intelligence: Educational implications (pp. 3–34). Basic Books.

Internal motivation - while money and status can be motivating factors, Goleman suggests that emotional intelligence is also predicated on an ability to work towards goals for internal reasons that supersede these more obvious benefits. Such motivations can include an inner vision or a place of purpose. The sheer joy of doing something pleasurable or even challenging, the curiosity and pleasure associated with learning, and the transcendent state that results from being immersed in an activity. Those that are internally motivated will have a propensity to pursue goals with energy and persistence, but also patience, retaining optimism even in the face of major challenges and setbacks.

Empathy - the ability to understand the emotional makeup of other people is an innate aspect of emotional intelligence, not least because it requires an ability to read between the lines, given that other people don't always directly reveal their emotions to us.

Social skills - this relates to the ability to build effective relationships and interact successfully with others. Central to this is the ability to find common ground for communication, which can help build rapport with others.

Goleman asserts that these separate components of emotional intelligence interact with one another to form what has commonly become referred to as EQ (emotional quotient). He firmly believes that emotional intelligence is critically important; not only in terms of experiencing happiness, but also with regard to reaching one's potential. Goleman, in fact, asserted that emotional intelligence is more important than cognitive intellect for predicting career success. While this assertion has been difficult to prove decisively, Goleman's view that too much emphasis historically has been placed on traditional predictors of employee performance has become far more accepted, while the value of emotional intelligence has been demonstrated in an array of studies.

For example, Mayer found in research conducted in 2004 that a variety of problematic behaviours, such as bullying, violence, tobacco use and drug problems, are far less likely to be present in those with high levels of emotional intelligence.[44] Another more recent study found that emotional intelligence correlates strongly with a broad range of skills, including decision-making, academic performance and achieving career goals.[45] Higher levels of emotional intelligence in children have even been linked with superior social competence from even the most tender age.[46]

Emotional intelligence also, as could be expected, has a profound impact on the quality of relationships that we

---

[44] https://www.jstor.org/stable/20447229

[45] https://www.verywellmind.com/components-of-emotional-intelligence-2795438

[46]https://www.researchgate.net/publication/256980706_Emotional_intelligence_in_the_first_5_years_of_life

experience. Research indicates that those with a high intelligence quotient are adept at managing emotions, and consequently enjoy improved interactions with friends. People scoring highly in emotional intelligence tests also tend to be perceived more positively by others.[47]

And, critically, emotional intelligence is associated with elevated levels of well-being and emotional satisfaction. Those with high EQ scores experienced lower levels of depression in one study, while the quality of high emotional intelligence has also been associated with enhanced life satisfaction and self-esteem.[48]

The good news is that these skills can be learned! There is little evidence that emotional intelligence is innate; rather it is something that we all have the potential to develop. Furthermore, Goleman has noted in his work that cognitive and emotional intelligence are not opposing qualities, two sides of the same coin, but rather complementary and collaborative. It is merely important to ensure that neither is neglected.

As a result of the work of Goleman and other researchers, the promotion and implementation of social and emotional learning in schools has become more prominent in recent years. In 2002, the United Nations Educational, Scientific and Cultural Organisation

---

[47] https://psycnet.apa.org/record/2008-12151-001
[48] *ibid.*

launched an international campaign to promote emotional learning in the classroom. This was based on 10 underlying principles that were heavily influenced by the work of Goleman, and his concept of emotional intelligence.

My takeaway from this has been that our ability to feel and connect with our emotions, to understand them, and then the ability to name them, can play a major role in leading a happy, fulfilling and successful life. To be able to observe our emotions and understand our feelings is the first step in building the emotional intelligence that we need in life. It helps to make us better and happier individuals overall, and from that initial foundation we can begin to assess how we manage our emotions and live with some of the difficulties that we encounter.

Vipassanā

I would like to elaborate on two key aspects of emotional intelligence: self-awareness and self-regulation. They are the foundations of emotional intelligence. You can only grow your emotional intelligence by first understanding your emotions and then learning to let them flow. You can only understand and manage the emotions of others once you have done this for yourself.

In 2019, my amazing husband Greg went on a Vipassanā meditation course. There, he learnt a technique to develop his self-awareness and self-regulation. Vipassanā is an Indian meditation technique. The term comes from the ancient language Pali and is often translated as "insight meditation". The practice helps you to gain insight about yourself, your emotions and on how we automatically operate and react to certain situations.

The practice is said to have been developed by Buddha himself more than 2,500 years ago. The technique in itself has nothing religious - it's a gymnastic of the mind... and of the body. It has been taught generations after generations, to monks in South and South-East Asia and was somehow preserved.

Greg needed a break. He had been close to burn out and felt like he had taught himself to ignore his unpleasant emotions. He describes his experience as putting his difficult feelings under a carpet, hoping they would disappear. But of course they would not, instead they would come back in repetitive thoughts, triggering unpleasant emotions. With high levels of stress at work he felt mentally exhausted. Also he started noticing that he was struggling to feel the more pleasant emotions - such as joy. Ignoring his emotions was not playing out as expected!

He describes Vipassana retreats as probably the most powerful kick-start to develop his own emotional intelligence. When you understand what is involved it's easy to understand The intensity of the experience. People who go to Vipassanā retreats learn and practise meditation for 10 days, 10 hours every day. Silence is strictly observed except for the guidance of the meditation teacher. It's not only demanding on the mind, it also places demands on the body, as you're sitting down meditating for this extended period of time.

I am fully aware that this practice will not be suitable for everyone, but people who engage in Vipassanā meditation often report transformative experiences. One comparative study, involving a Vipassanā retreat, found that those who engaged in the Vipassanā programme reported significantly improved physical and psychological well-being.[49] And this was very much the case with my husband. The experience changed his life and state of being.

---

[49] https://www.ncbi.nlm.nih.gov/pmc/articles/PMC3174711/

The good news is that you can learn similar practices to steadily grow your emotional intelligence by yourself. I will use a metaphor to explain - imagine you are training two wings of a bird. The first wing is the ability to observe your body. Our emotions are all expressed through our bodies in the form of energy. When you are scared, your heart may pause or accelerate; when you feel joy, your forehead may widen and you may smile. In coaching we say that emotions are e-motions, or energy in motions. Training the first wing consists of learning to observe this flow of energy in your body.

Some of us do this intuitively, for others it is harder. Like Greg you may have taught yourself to ignore your unpleasant emotions, you may have developed a 'thick skin' and desensitised yourself. If this does not come naturally, the best way to train this mental muscle is to practice a body scan meditation. Spend 10 or more minutes sitting comfortably with your back straight, eyes closed, feeling one after the other, the different parts of your body. You can search online for "body scan", on most mediation applications, to find various guided meditations on this. As you develop this skill, you will start to more powerfully and automatically and naturally feel your emotions as they arise.

At first, this was actually difficult for Greg because he started feeling more, including the emotions he had tried to avoid in the past. That's where the second wing comes in. It's called equanimity, or the ability to observe your emotions *without judgement*. This does not mean that you stop appreciating your moments of joy and happiness. All the opposite. Because the only way to remove judgement is to be fully curious about your emotions and how they express themselves in your body.

You learn to apply your curiosity equally to your pleasant and to your unpleasant emotions such as anger, sadness and fear. To develop this skill, each time you feel a strong emotion, observe with complete curiosity and wonder how it manifests itself in your body. Do you feel tense in the shoulder? Do you feel your breathing becoming more shallow? Just pay attention to your bodily sensations. Start with emotions that you can accept easily and as you grow this mental muscle, apply it to the more difficult or powerful emotions. By doing this, you will learn to stay fully present in the moment.

Through this practice, you learn to appreciate your emotions as passing signals that inform you. This helps you grow your awareness of what triggers you, positively or negatively. By observing yourself being triggered, you are not unconsciously reacting anymore. You are now aware and able to make a choice on your next actions. This is a lifetime practice. Greg has not become a Buddha yet, but he is much more able to appreciate the joyful moments and accept and let go of the difficult ones.

Just as attending that Vipassanā retreat required courage from my husband; to pause and to acknowledge the balance that your life requires will also require bravery. It necessitates a willingness to look inside yourself, and it can be challenging. It can be scary. Often there is fear associated with the process. And that's why a lot of people will avoid peering into their emotions at all costs. They will go about their everyday lives, putting their hands over their eyes and moving forwards determinedly, because that's sometimes easier than assessing the way that they feel deep down. It's a form of self-protection.

Nature

Recently, I was reading a book on the practice of Shinrin-Yoku. This translates in English to the phrase 'forest bathing'. This has become a popular cultural practice in Japan, although it is not one of their more ancient traditions, having first emerged in the 1980s. But Shinrin-Yoku is so powerful and compelling that it has become a way of life for many Japanese people.

The ethos behind it is quite simple. Get away from the hectic pace of life, slow down, pause, appreciate nature, and enjoy the sheer beauty of our surroundings. Take a little time to explore yourself and the forest mindfully, and reconnect with the natural world. Being mindful means being present with the colours, the smells, the sights and sounds of nature.

Taking the time to reconnect with nature and sometimes even experience the most elemental, simple things in a truly connected fashion is hugely important. Just being in the moment without other things going on. Enjoying a meal. Listening to music. Observing the natural world around you. Living in the moment.

This all helps slow the mind down and create a connection between yourself and nature, which in turn helps you to just be in that moment. This can be the bridge that you need to begin truly appreciating and loving yourself.

It's been proven that being in nature has a positive effect on the well-being of both body and mind. As with so many things that just feel intrinsically good for us, there is scientific support for the idea that both shinrin-yoku and being in nature generally offer health benefits. In fact, Lisa Nisbet, PhD, a psychologist at Trent University in Ontario, Canada, told the American Psychological Association in an interview that the supporting evidence for this is significant and growing:

"There is mounting evidence, from dozens and dozens of researchers, that nature has benefits for both physical and psychological human well-being. You can boost your mood just by walking in nature, even in urban nature. And the sense of connection you have with the natural world seems to contribute to happiness even when you're not physically immersed in nature,[50]" Nisbet commented.

For example, a meta-analysis published in the Environmental Research journal found that spending time in green space reduces vulnerability to chronic illnesses. It is believed that the phytochemicals emitted by trees, which are inhaled by humans, contribute to this phenomenon, with some studies even suggesting that phytochemicals play a role in increasing the existence of 'killer' cells in the human immune system.[51]

The meta-analysis was a very significant piece of research, not least due to its sheer scope; 103 observational studies and 40 interventional studies were

---

[50] https://www.apa.org/monitor/2020/04/nurtured-nature
[51] https://www.ncbi.nlm.nih.gov/pmc/articles/PMC2793341/

used, encompassing 290 million participants spread across 20 countries. The study also discovered that spending time in green spaces lowered cortisol levels - a stress hormone - along with a reduced risk of coronary heart disease, lowered blood pressure and cholesterol, and diminished the risk of type II diabetes.[52]

Aside from the phytochemical factor, green spaces also tend to result in physical activity, social interaction, exposure to sunlight, and reduced pollution, all of which have physical benefits. Consequently, some researchers and experts believe that 'green prescriptions' could play a role in improving health outcomes for those who spend the majority of their time in urban areas.

This is an increasingly important factor, as the number of people residing in cities is growing and set to expand further. According to the United Nations Population Division, by 2050 around 75% of the world's population will live in cities. This means that nature deficit disorder – the concept that human beings are spending less time outdoors, and that this results in a wide range of behavioural, physical and psychological problems - is becoming an increasingly common constituent of contemporary life.[53]

---

[52] https://www.sciencedirect.com/science/article/pii/S0013935118303323
[53] https://www.un.org/development/desa/en/news/population/2018-world-urbanization-prospects.html

This has implications for many of us, particularly as the more the experience and impact of nature are explored, the more evidence researchers find for their multiplicity of benefits. For example, one study of forest bathing conducted with middle-aged Tokyo office workers discovered that after regular walks in the forest participants were less anxious and enjoyed improved sleep quality.[54] Another study from the same researcher found that this pronounced benefit of physical activity in nature could not be imitated elsewhere; Li found that only the experience of walking in a forest improved people's vigour and reduced fatigue.[55]

Here are some other examples of studies supporting the benefits of connecting with nature:

- In 2017, an extensive review of academic literature noted that the overwhelming majority of human history has been spent living in nature, and therefore it is entirely logical that we should find this a natural and pleasing environment in which to spend time. The review concluded that "the practice offers humans an authentic way of healing and health prevention for the mind, body and spirit".[56]

---

[54] https://www.ncbi.nlm.nih.gov/pmc/articles/PMC3216244/

[55] https://www.mdpi.com/1660-4601/11/7/7207/htm

[56] https://www.ncbi.nlm.nih.gov/pmc/articles/PMC5580555/

- And empirical research on Shinrin-Yoku demonstrated that "forest bathing activities might have the following merits: remarkably improving cardiovascular function, hemodynamic indexes, neuroendocrine indexes, metabolic indexes, immunity and inflammatory indexes, antioxidant indexes, and electrophysiological indexes; significantly enhancing people's emotional state, attitude, and feelings towards things, physical and psychological recovery, and adaptive behaviours; and obvious alleviation of anxiety and depression."[57]

- Another systematic review and meta-analysis of forest bathing carried out in 2019 found that forest bathing consistently reduced cortisol levels in those participating [58] and that *"Shinrin-Yoku can be effective in reducing mental health symptoms in the short term, particularly anxiety."*[59]

There are many more resources and research around the benefits of spending time in nature. Here are several examples:

---

[57]https://environhealthprevmed.biomedcentral.com/articles/10.1186/s121 99-019-0822-8

[58] https://pubmed.ncbi.nlm.nih.gov/31001682/

[59] https://link.springer.com/article/10.1007/s11469-020-00363-4

Cognitive benefits - Research from the University of Michigan found that walking in nature resulted in increased memory compared to walking around a city.[60] Another study from the University of Chicago discovered that green spaces near schools promote cognitive development in children and green views near children's homes promote self-control behaviours.[61] Researchers also found that students who spent time in a garden before conducting a task requiring attention had higher levels of concentration.[62]

Happiness and well-being - Participants in a Finnish study from 2014 felt psychologically restored after just 15 minutes of sitting in nature, while the results were even more pronounced when they spent time walking as well. Elsewhere, a representative sample of 20,000 UK adults found that people who had spent at least 2 recreational hours in nature during the previous week reported significantly greater health and well-being. This applied across all demographics and regardless of the initial health of the participants.[63]

Eases depression - Multiple studies have documented the fact that walking in nature can help reduce depression.

---

[60]https://www.spring.org.uk/2009/01/memory-improved-20-by-nature-walk.php

[61] https://journals.sagepub.com/doi/10.1177/0963721419854100

[62]https://www.sciencedirect.com/science/article/abs/pii/S0272494415000328?via%3Dihub

[63] https://www.nature.com/articles/s41598-019-44097-3

This included one study from 2015, which found that spending time in nature reduces rumination and subgenual prefrontal cortex activation - both associated with bouts of lowered mood. "Participants who went on a 90-min walk through a natural environment reported lower levels of rumination and showed reduced neural activity in an area of the brain linked to risk for mental illness compared with those who walked through an urban environment."[64]

Other benefits associated with daily connections and walks in nature include weight loss (associated with being outside more), increased vitamin D (through exposure to sunlight), better overall health and immune system. A study from Harvard University demonstrated that exposing people to natural light led to faster healing post surgery.[65]

In conclusion, it is clear that spending time in nature is hugely beneficial for health on multiple levels, and that Shinrin-Yoku, or forest bathing, is a practice that can help both psychologically and physically. With this in mind, I encourage you to set aside some quality moments to spend in nature. It's pleasurable and the research shows that such practices are particularly valuable at a time like

---

[64] https://pubmed.ncbi.nlm.nih.gov/26124129/

[65] https://www.health.harvard.edu/press_releases/spending-time-outdoors-is-good-for-you

this, when many of us are a little sore, a little bruised, and need to recuperate.

"Look deep into nature, and then you will understand everything better." - *Albert Einstein*

7. "Wear sunscreen"

When I coach, I do not "know", I don't dispense advice, I listen, I am deeply and truly curious for my clients, and I challenge their thought patterns to trigger new perspectives and gain clarity on a situation.

But sometimes I come across a resource that truly inspires me, and that I wish the world could read, so If I had to choose one text to share with my children, with my loved ones it would be this one:

"If I could offer you only one tip for the future, sunscreen would be it. The long-term benefits of sunscreen have been proved by scientists, whereas the rest of my advice has no basis more reliable than my own meandering experience. I will dispense this advice now.

Enjoy the power and beauty of your youth. Oh, never mind. You will not understand the power and beauty of your youth until they've faded. But trust me, in 20 years, you'll look back at photos of yourself and recall in a way you can't grasp now how much possibility lay before you and how fabulous you really looked. You are not as fat as you imagine.

Don't worry about the future. Or worry, but know that worrying is as effective as trying to solve an algebra equation by chewing bubble gum. The real troubles in your life are apt to be things that never crossed your worried mind, the kind that blindside you at 4pm on some idle Tuesday.

Do one thing every day that scares you.

Sing.

Don't be reckless with other people's hearts. Don't put up with people who are reckless with yours.

Floss.

Don't waste your time on jealousy. Sometimes you're ahead, sometimes you're behind. The race is long and, in the end, it's only with yourself.

Remember the compliments you receive. Forget the insults. If you succeed in doing this, tell me how.

Keep your old love letters. Throw away your old bank statements.

Stretch.

Don't feel guilty if you don't know what you want to do with your life. The most interesting people I know didn't know at 22 what they wanted to do with their lives. Some of the most interesting 40-year-olds I know still don't.

Get plenty of calcium. Be kind to your knees. You'll miss them when they're gone.

Maybe you'll marry, maybe you won't. Maybe you'll have children, maybe you won't. Maybe you'll divorce at 40, maybe you'll dance the funky chicken on your 75th wedding anniversary. Whatever you do, don't congratulate yourself too much, or berate yourself either. Your choices are half chance. So are everybody else's.

Enjoy your body. Use it every way you can. Don't be afraid of it or of what other people think of it. It's the greatest instrument you'll ever own.

Dance, even if you have nowhere to do it but your living room.

Read the directions, even if you don't follow them.

Do not read beauty magazines. They will only make you feel ugly.

Get to know your parents. You never know when they'll be gone for good. Be nice to your siblings. They're your best link to your past and the people most likely to stick with you in the future.

Understand that friends come and go, but with a precious few you should hold on. Work hard to bridge the gaps in geography and lifestyle, because the older you get, the more you need the people who knew you when you were young.

Live in New York City once, but leave before it makes you hard. Live in Northern California once, but leave before it makes you soft. Travel.

Accept certain inalienable truths: Prices will rise. Politicians will philander. You, too, will get old. And when you do, you'll fantasise that when you were young, prices were reasonable, politicians were noble and children respected their elders.

Respect your elders.

Don't expect anyone else to support you. Maybe you have a trust fund. Maybe you'll have a wealthy spouse. But you never know when either one might run out.

Don't mess too much with your hair or by the time you're 40 it will look 85.

Be careful whose advice you buy, but be patient with those who supply it. Advice is a form of nostalgia. Dispensing it is a way of fishing the past from the disposal, wiping it off, painting over the ugly parts and recycling it for more than it's worth.

But trust me on the sunscreen."

Mary Schmich

Well done, for taking the time to pause and to reflect.

Once you've lowered the noise in your head and allowed yourself to slow down and BE just for a while - the time will come when the urge to move will pick you up again.

When you are ready, once you feel the energy is "back", listen to the signal - the time to bounce back has come.

Before you do so, anchor in your life and in your mind, what you have learned from slowing down, and what new practices you want to incorporate in your life ahead. Cultivate your positive space, your self-love, and keep connecting to nature and to your body and mind.

Once you are back in balance, and can feel your energy tank is fuller, let's look ahead and bounce back into life, with joy, energy and purpose.

Part III
Bouncing back

8. Choosing

Today, as we emerge from the crux of the pandemic, I feel a little sluggish, a little weary, and I have a deep urge for a soothing and joyful period in my life. I crave lightness, friends, fun and spontaneous laughter. I want to dance, to be spontaneous, to rid myself of restrictions, prescriptions and inhibitions. To feel alive. I know that I am far from alone in wanting all of these things to occur, and I've experienced this repeatedly with my clients.

Confidence & boundaries

I often work with my clients on the confidence to say "no", and for that matter having the confidence to say "yes" as well. We've been in a highly pressurised situation, but one in which choice was essentially eliminated. And now gradually, choice is part of our lives once more. So many aspects of our lives are indeed focused on choice, on the abundance of opportunity and feeling like you are choosing and not being told what to do is key.

The crux of this choice is essentially based on what you wish to accumulate and experience in your life. The first thing to establish is that we have the power of the affirmative; we can say "yes", even if the process of saying "yes" isn't always easy.

What is it that you wish to encounter in greater abundance?

What aspects of social life will you embrace?

Which relationships will you nurture?

What priorities will you invest time and energy in the coming months?

What will you say "yes" to?

Equally, when we have the confidence to say "no", the confidence to define situations that are undesirable, or roles for which we feel unprepared, we establish important boundaries. Boundaries can be difficult to position and to manage, particularly if we are caring, warm and want to support others.

Not all of our relationships are healthy and sometimes you need to protect yourself and your well-being. There is a place where discontinuing these disruptive and debilitating relationships is simply the healthiest decision. What lockdowns have essentially provided us with is the opportunity to detox some of our relationships, and potentially dissolve any that are creating toxicity.

What are the boundaries that you want to define?

How will you respect them?

How will you ensure they are respected by others?

What will you say no to?

Setting boundaries is an act of self-love and self-respect. People who respect you will understand that - and sometimes they might need guidance to see where the boundary is. Be open, share, teach them what your needs are, and what you are willing to accept or not. Respect yourself, set your boundaries and others will respect them in return.

"Setting boundaries isn't a way to get rid of people, but a way to keep them in your life without destroying your inner peace" [66].

---

[66] Vex King, Healing Is the New High - 2021

The connections

Personally, I've benefited from recognising the people that mean a lot to me. The relationships that are there for me when it really counts showed up. Helping deliver food to my front door when I was in quarantine, or assisting me when my son was suffering with Covid. There was a noticeable demarcation between the brave people who were invested in our relationship, and those who evidently felt disconnected and even indifferent.

It's the opportunity to pick quality relationships going forward, as opposed to quantity that makes the difference. It has also become clear to me that the longer-term friendships that I have, which perhaps date back to my youth, are important. Perhaps they take a little more nurturing due to distance, perhaps we have to navigate different geographical regions and locations, but I've found that we stuck together during this difficult time, and that this has strengthened the bond of these friendships.

Human connections have been put under pressure, and even severed completely, during the pandemic lockdown. People have been forced to literally shut their front doors and lock themselves away from human contact. Not only the people that matter most to them - friends and loved ones - but even social contact as a whole ceased for some people.

We mentioned Maslow in an earlier chapter, and his hierarchy of needs, which established the concept that contact with other human beings is essential for our psychological, and even physical, well-being[67]. Once our basic survival and safety needs have been met, our next most fundamental requirement is to build and foster relationships with other people.

Scientific research has solidly backed this impression. Research from 2014 found that students experienced greater happiness and increased feelings of belonging on days when they interacted with more classmates than usual; ie. not necessarily people with whom they had particularly strong or established relationships.[68]

And in a study published in the Journal of Social Behaviour, Umberson and Montez noted that "solid scientific evidence shows that social relationships affect a range of health outcomes, including mental health, physical health, health habits, and mortality risk." The research went on to note that the "confluence of smaller families, high divorce rates, employment-related geographical mobility, and population ageing means that adults of all ages, and in particular the elderly, will be at

---

[67] McLeod, Dr., S. (2020). Maslow's Hierarchy of Needs. Simple Psychology.
[68] Sandstrom, G. & Dunn, E. (2014). Social Interactions and Well-Being: The Surprising Power of Weak Ties. Personality and Social Psychology Bulletin.

increasing risk of social isolation and shrinking family ties in the future."[69]

And yet the factors that the authors cite as being significant are collectively of a relatively small scale and scope compared to the total lockdown of society. It therefore naturally follows that the psychological impact of Covid-19 will be far greater.

As we begin to emerge from the unnatural state that has been imposed on us, many people will face difficulties. But the nature of those difficulties will differ greatly depending on the person. For example, there could well be a dichotomy between introverts and extroverts. It's even possible that some introverts have found the lockdowns to be life-affirming, enabling them to invest energy in pastimes that they wouldn't have time to engage in usually, while being less affected by the state of social seclusion. While introverts still need people, they gain energy from spending time alone, making coping with being alone relatively easier.

Conversely, extroverts channel energy from being in contact with other people, which means that the weight of being sequestered alone in their house, could have weighed on them heavily. There is no right or wrong answer, nor state of being, but it is important to acknowledge where you are in the process. Just as we all

---

[69] Umberson, D. & Montez, J. (2010). Social Relationships and Health: A Flashpoint for Health Policy. Journal of Health and Social Behavior.

occupy different places on the introvert / extrovert spectrum, so we are all emerging from the lockdowns in different places as well.

Recently, when working with Alexandra, she realised that as a natural introvert and full time working mother of 3 children, she had greatly suffered from the lack of personal space during the pandemic. She had a deep urge of space, of silence, of being alone. The lack of these things during the previous 2 years fed a feeling of unhappiness and an overall sense of loss of direction. She discussed this with her husband and brought the topic to work, and together they all backed her to take a break. A 5 months break from work, and a few days break from family obligations. This gave her a gasp of air, and allowed her to reconnect with herself, and with the energy and joy she had inside. It allowed her to bounce back in a purposeful way. It came as a surprise to her to realise, it was ok to ask for a break and that her world would support her in finding her ground again. Of course, not everyone is able to do that, and a break to rebalance might take many different shapes for different individuals. However, the first step is the same - it's an awareness of your need, and then it's having the courage to act on that need, and to ask for support to make it happen.

> *"What is the bravest thing you've ever said?" asked the boy.*
>
> *"Asking for help," said the horse.*[70]

I've noticed that the lockdowns have been such an arid desert of disconnection for many people that the prospect of returning to the oasis of human relationships can even seem unsettling. What used to come naturally now seems awkward, and we're not quite sure how to go about it. How do we arrange that informal drink or lunch with a friend, when this hasn't been part of our usual experience for such a long time?

If you've encountered these difficulties then you're not alone. This has been the prevailing experience for millions of people all over the world. No matter how natural and desirable human interaction may seem, particularly after being cooped up and isolated for many months, making this transition has been far from facile. So in this section of the book, we're going to address this important issue.

---

[70] The Boy, The Mole, The Fox and The Horse – 2019, by Charlie Mackesy

Reflections on reconnections

Most of us will have missed some connections dearly, but now that we have the opportunity to rebuild them, where should we start? And how should we go about it? In many ways, emerging from the pandemic is as daunting as the lockdowns themselves, and many people are undermined by a gnawing uncertainty regarding the whole process.

Let's consider a few questions to trigger your thinking.

Take each question in turn, and instinctively note down the first names that come to mind. Once you've captured one of a few words or names for each, come back to the initial question and redraft a more thoughtful response.

What is a meaningful way for you to reconnect with your loved ones?

Which relationships will you investigate and rebuild?

Which relationships have you lost due to the pandemic?

Which relationships are you ready to let go?

Which friendships have emerged, or been strengthened, and you are now ready to invest in?

9. Filling up the energy tank

Body energy

As I take the time to heal and choose how I want to move forward, I found that it was liberating to be able to take care of myself - my body, my mind, my heart. And the more that I was able to take care of myself, the more I found that my energy levels were replenished, and that I could look to the future with optimism.

It can sometimes be difficult to cut through all of the noise. There is a huge amount of advice and information circulating nowadays, with podcasts, blogs, YouTube channels, and the mainstream media. This can make it tricky to know how to bounce back. I think an excellent place to begin is simply listening to your heart. This can help you decide what is right for you, and once you have made this decision, you can then arrange your life so that you make space for this and prioritise it.

For me it began with feeling healthy. We all have different ways of achieving this, but I'm not a particularly sporty person, so some impressive sporting feat was out of the question! Instead, I set myself a daily target in terms of steps, and reconnected with yoga. I find the latter both relaxing and restorative for myself, while ensuring that I walk around on a daily basis simply gets me moving and feeling active again. Just simply moving can make a difference; suddenly you're not wallowing in a negative state any longer.

Additionally, there was also a pampering aspect to the process. I required some time to relax, to comfort myself, and take care of the feminine side of my life, which had been somewhat neglected during the pandemic. I'd almost locked the womanly side of myself behind the doors of my house for months on end, and now I wanted that important component of my being to flower again.

The third aspect of this health-driven reboot was to focus attention on what goes into my body. We are what we eat, and thus I've ensured that I'm particularly careful with diet. It's important to me that the fuel that I give to my body is of the highest quality. It's not necessarily about purchasing expensive or indulgent food, more about going back to basics and attempting to remove chemicals from my diet as much as possible. Reconnecting my body to a more natural way of life.

In this regard, a whole foods diet is almost universally believed by nutritionists to be superior to one containing a significant amount of processed food. On one level, this is quite straightforward; as I just mentioned, this is simply more natural. It's close to how our ancestors ate, and consequently we're much more evolved to eat this way as well.

But there is more to it than this. Foods are processed for a variety of reasons, not least to make them more appealing to us. Our bodies crave sugar, salt and fat, as historically these nutrients were scarce, and anything that packed in energy was valuable. That is not the case today, where in part of the world, there is an ever-growing obesity and diabetes epidemic which proves that food is not scarce, but that healthy diets are.

Whole foods tend to be nutrient-dense whereas processed foods are usually calorie-dense. And the artificial preservatives, flavourings and colourings included in processed food have been linked with a variety of adverse side-effects, both relatively trivial and serious. Not all additives are bad, but as a general rule it's better to consume food that doesn't contain a vast list of ingredients. The British Medical Journal has published two important population studies that corroborate this impression. The first found that "higher consumption of ultra-processed foods was associated with higher risks of cardiovascular, coronary heart, and cerebrovascular diseases."[71] And the second concluded that "higher consumption of ultra-processed foods was independently associated with a 62% relatively increased hazard for all cause mortality. For each additional serving of ultra-processed food, all cause mortality increased by 18%."[72]

---

[71] https://www.bmj.com/content/365/bmj.l1451
[72] https://www.bmj.com/content/365/bmj.l1949

Two further studies also provided interesting insight. The first showed that eating a diet based on whole foods can be an effective way to treat depression. As a result the researchers involved asserted that an intake of an anti-inflammatory diet; magnesium and folic acid; various fatty acids; and fish consumption is the ideal dietary approach to relieving depression. The study concludes that "on the public health nurse's preventative and health-promoting work, support and assistance with changing people's dietary habits may be effective in promoting depression."

Another study suggested that one reason issues related to diet, obesity and diabetes have not been effectively addressed is that interventions have been focused on removing "nutrients of concern", rather than delivering a holistic and healthy diet plan - such as moving to whole foods or plant-based diets.[73]

I am not a nutritionist and there is a huge amount of published research on this subject. I've simply noticed that tweaking your diet to something more healthy and natural is certainly something worth considering.

---

[73]https://bmcmedicine.biomedcentral.com/articles/10.1186/s12916-021-01984-9

The power of a happy and positive mind

Putting all of these relatively simple things together can be hugely valuable and have a beneficial impact that may exceed your imagination. Once you've taken care of your body, you can also concentrate some attention on your mind as well. We discussed the value of taking a break from your day previously, how engaging in some meditation can be beneficial, but you also need to nurture your mental processes. Reading, writing, learning, feeling alive in my mind, being challenged and stretched intellectually is an important part of this process for myself. And it's from this that I derive a lot of energy, when I can feel my brain being stimulated. It has an almost symbiotic impact on my body, and I get the sensation of wanting to move, wanting to experience life again.

As we've discussed previously, there needs to be a balance between being and doing. When I was able to cultivate and nourish my curiosity with information, it opened up my purpose in life. My interest was pricked and my curiosity was triggered. It can be difficult to get yourself going again after such a time of virtual hibernation; it's almost as if your body becomes a malfunctioning engine in a car that has been shut away in the garage for too long.

One central path of self-care that is important to me is connecting to joy. Connecting to happiness, connecting to a positive mindset. I'm a great believer that happiness is something that provides colour to my life, making it more enjoyable and valuable. But it's not something to be taken for granted. I strongly believe that happiness doesn't just hit you, it's not freely handed out. It has to be earned. Feeling joy and happiness is something that we have to work on, and it's something that I personally cultivate every single day. Of course some of us are born with, and benefit from, a much easier ride than others, but I've observed that this does not necessarily give them an easier access to inner happiness.

As part of this process, I fully appreciate that there are different levels of happiness. The first level is the small joys in life, the simple, everyday things that create glee in our hearts. It could be walking through a meadow of blooming flowers, or having a close moment with a child reading a book, or a moment of spontaneous laughter. Any number of little things that make us feel warm inside, and imbue the days of our lives with a more pleasing array of watercolours.

I believe that creating these moments is critical to happiness, and even just basic good health. So I have mindfully decided to enable myself to create more of these small moments of joy. And the more that I pursue these, the more that I start to feel that my life is spontaneous, fun, unplanned, and full of elation. It didn't happen overnight, but it's akin to a stone rolling down a hill; if you stick with the process, it soon begins to gather momentum.

In many ways, the pandemic was tough. I certainly missed out on a lot of experiences that I would have enjoyed, and even taken for granted normally, such as children's parties and milestones with my kids. There were lots of adult things as well, with birthdays, weddings, anniversaries, and other moments of celebration and rejoicing conspicuous by their absence. When the onerous conditions of the lockdowns began to be eased, I reflected that I needed to create more of these sorts of experiences. I had to allow them to seep back into my life.

For example, I attended my cousin's wedding in France, when there were still quarantine rules in place in the UK. I remember that everyone thought I was crazy to go to all that trouble, just for a couple of days, and then be confined to my own home for 10 days on return. But I felt such an urge to feel that love and happiness, and to have the experience of dancing under the bright blue sky and sunshine meant that it was worth every single moment and inconvenience involved.

Naturally, some people are better equipped from birth to access this state, but even their happiness is neither guaranteed nor permanent. This sense of happiness and fulfilment is something that we work towards. It's not in stasis; it's something that is developing and evolving. Those among us who work harder at it are more likely to find it, as it requires resilience and effort. It's not necessarily something that comes easily, but I believe that the work is definitely worth it.

What small pleasure brings you joy?

When was the last time you felt deeply happy?

What makes you laugh?

What could you do in the next week that would bring you a feeling of happiness?

How can you weave in more happy moments in your daily life?

Gratefulness

I regularly encourage a daily practice of gratefulness to my clients and loved ones. I find this practice of gratitude increases my happiness and my overall energy to embrace life and what it throws at me. Working with our positive thoughts is like building a muscle; I regularly work on it with my children, and the more they practice the easier it gets. Experts in positive psychology have shown that even if it is not always easily accessible, a regular practice helps "rewire" our brains into a more positive spiral.[74] From there, we have access to our resourcefulness, energy and feelings of joy and happiness.

The bigger our gratitude jar, the more resources we'll have to tap into when facing challenging times. Research has shown that it makes us more resilient to face adversity, change, and unwanted challenges.

To practice ask yourself:

What am I grateful for?

---

[74] The Little Book of Happiness: Simple Practices for a Good Life - 2019 by Miriam Akhtar

What else? Dig deeper and access what is at the essence of your gratefulness right now.

What's positive in my life today?

Who am I grateful to?

What are the good things that I have right under my nose that I have gotten used to?

Find your own 2 or 3 powerful questions, and make it a ritual practice before falling asleep, or as you wake in the morning.

For me - this beautiful poem or mediation from Sarah Blondin, never fails to take me there. I feel emotions, but a deep sense of gratitude and strength after connecting with her honouring of life.

I invite you to either connect to an audio device and use the link below, listen to Sarah's voice, or read them. If you prefer to read these to yourself, I invite you to ensure you have 6 - 7 minutes ahead of you, settle down in a quiet and comfortable space, and read these words aloud. Let them resonate in the space, take your time, it's a poem, the words flow and as poetry does, it invites a dreamy and reflective space.

By Sarah Blondin

Listen to this beautiful meditation:
https://insighttimer.com/sarahblondin/guided-meditations/honoring-life

"To my lover, my husband, my wife, my child, my dearest friend, my mentor.

To the stranger I pass on the street. The kind eyes who met mine.

The gentle breath shared while being embraced.

To the ear that listened and held my words as precious.

To the ones who stand with me in this lifetime.

To the life that comes rising along with the sun,

that opens my eyes, that floods my body with vitality and vigour.

To the love that spills from light, the love that falls from the seams in my clothing.

To the abundance that fills the cup of clean water I drink.

To the fighting, the warring, the violent storms that crash within me, and around me.

To the ones that come to help show me what hurts, in order to be healed.

To the people who are on this healing journey with me, that are not allowing me to stay small,

but are forcing growth to come bursting forth from the wound that binds us together.

To the remembering of who I am.

To the glimpses of my formless beauty, my unstoried self.

To the remembering, and then forgetting again.

To the cycle, and circle, and dance with essence, and all that is not.

To the heartbeat of my humanity, the tenderness of learning to walk without hands to hold.

To the gentle, most incredulous journey we are all on.

To the breaking free from our painful, conditional joy and happiness.

To loving someone and needing nothing in return.

To the giving of yourself to the fires that come to burn your restrictive walls to ash.

To the coming home. And leaving. And coming home, again.

To the fear found in my clenched fists, my sore shoulders, my shallow breath.

The gilded knot in my stomach.

To the fear that seizes the homes of the places within me

that are not aligned with my intrinsic self.

To the fear that is there to remind me, relentlessly, of the places

I need to open my eyes, the places I need to love.

The places that made me forget who I was,

before I learned to clench against it all.

To the dark nights, the relief of the moon,

the soft earth that forms to cradle the shape of my foot.

To the crickets and the birds who sing our world into harmony,

To the flowers that wish to sit on my windowsill,

the trees that grow to reach the most sunlight.

To the grass that sways, and soothes.

To the webs the spider tirelessly builds overnight,

only to be torn down in the light of day.

To the life that pulses in exaltation below my feet, every day that I'm alive.

To the portal it offers into remembrance of our wholeness.

To our source of unconditional love.

To the beauty that comes from hitting the rocks at the bottom of the well.

To the surrender that comes after I have been squeezed of my last drop of control.

To the overwhelming freedom that lives there behind everything I diligently carry.

To the wealth that waits for me to turn my gaze toward it.

To the gift of letting go. To the outstretching of palms.

To the laying down of arms.

To the miracles born of not doing, but being.

To the unclaimed love we are all blundering toward.

To the gravitational pull that constantly tugs us towards centre,

even when we are screaming in the other direction.

To the constant unearthing of who we are.

To the waxing and waning, to the groaning, and roaring.

To the discoveries that blaze.

To our valiance, our fortitude, our constant learning.

To our courageous, beautiful selves.

To the purity of who we are, the mighty force we were born as.

To the vulnerable, most magnificent heart in our chest.

To the world of wonder, shrouded in every soul.

To the simple, the plain, ordinary life I get to live...

I would like to say, 'Thank You'.

I would like to share my most sincere gratitude, and love,

and appreciation to the simple, the plain, the ordinary life I get to live.

I would like to say a most sincere thank you,

for all of this glory that waits for me to turn my gaze toward it.

I thank you. I love you. I thank you.

Close your eyes. And let these recognitions be what you carry close,

as you rise and fall throughout your day.

Let these recognitions anchor you to the love that is yours,

that is waiting, that you are infused with.

Let yourself be reminded that everything is a gift.

A raucous, riotous, astonishing gift for you to revel in.

There is no right and wrong, no good and bad, no must-be's. This is it.

It is a tale of fervent love. A tale of how you learn to discover the immense beauty living inside of you. Breath. Hold your heart. Take a deep inhale and exhale.

Go forth dearest love, into the great pilgrimage of your life, and offer your most sincerest thanks for all of this. For all that is. For all of the glory that waits for you to turn your gaze toward it."

10. Looking ahead

As we gradually ease back into post-Covid-19 reality, we'll need to re-adjust and find our balance again. I believe that having the privilege of looking ahead can play a major role in our well-being. Again, there is a balance to be struck here, between living in the moment and working towards a distant horizon. I know I am working towards big plans and projects that provide me with a sense of direction. We are goal-oriented creatures, and if you have something that you're working towards, it offers you a purpose that nourishes you, and encourages you to get out of bed in the morning.

It doesn't have to be something monumental, some grand plan or scheme. It could be something as simple as planning for a holiday in the next year or so, or it could be related to your professional life. The important thing is that it has value and meaning for yourself as an individual. This will be such a liberating process at a time when we've put all of our plans and schemes on hold. Allowing them to come back into my life, being brave enough to plan and look ahead, was an important part of recuperation and recovery for me, even though I know that there is some inherent uncertainty involved. Having a sense of direction and feeling the joy associated with the basic process of planning was a medicine that my body needed.

Working from home has become the new norm in my world, seeing my clients on video calls, and working with groups online and through the magic of breakout rooms. Although it took time to adjust and empower that space, I have become used to it, and now I find that I enjoy it. But I now have to readjust, consider travelling to run face-to-face workshops, and see my clients in the flesh. What a gift for someone like me who loves people, feeling with them, and holding a precious and truthful space by being in the same room. At the same time, I will have to become accustomed to seeing my children less, to give up school drops and some pickups. I won't have my post-it notes around my computer to support me on a new programme, or my lunch breaks with my husband in the garden. The whole scope of my work will look and feel different.

Once again, change is happening. I am embracing it, eyes wide open. It's a new challenge and I want to rethink my balance, my ikigai, my plan, so that this readjustment goes as smoothly as possible.

Ikigai

To keep pushing the reflection and move forward in a thoughtful way I find the Japanese model "Ikigai" a powerful tool. The Oxford English Dictionary defines ikigai as "a motivating force; something or someone that gives a person a sense of purpose or a reason for living". More generally it may refer to something that brings pleasure or fulfilment. The term is based on 2 Japanese words: iki (生き), meaning 'life; alive, and kai (甲斐,) meaning: an effect, a result, a benefit, to arrive at a reason for living, a meaning to life, something that makes life worth living; a raison d'être'.

Ikigai is often expressed via 4 overlapping circles:

75

These 4 circles represent what you love, what you're good at, what the world needs, and what you can be paid for. Passion, mission, profession, vocation. The underlying

---

75 Francesc Miralles - Find your Ikigai. BODETREE, based on the work of Mark Winn "What is your Ikigai?"

principle is to reconnect with what matters to you, and be mindful about this in your everyday life.

An example related to ikigai came up in my coaching recently. Charlotte needed to find a greater sense of purpose in her life, her work, and even her family. She sensed an urge to understand the direction of her life, to feel an underlying sense of purpose and motivation. We began to discuss the direction that her life would take in the future. She had lost her sense of self during the pandemic, and needed to rediscover her zest for life. There were a variety of techniques and principles that could have been utilised here, but I particularly value this Japanese concept of ikigai. Together we explored each dimension, in a rational and systematic way.

Explore your own ikigai by drawing the overlapping circles and answering the following questions:

What do you love ?

What are you good at?

What can you do that would generate income?

What do you feel the world needs?

Digging deeper in each circle -

What are the things you love and what you are good at?
(In this overlap you will find passion.)

What are you good at that you can get paid for? (This overlap is where you're most likely to see where your profession sits.)

What do you feel the world needs that you could act on and be paid for? (This overlap is where you're most likely to find your vocation.)

What do you love and that you feel the world needs? (This overlap will encompass your mission.)

Take your time with each dimension: draw, pencil, erase, start again.

It can be a messy process and that's ok. Know that in the centre where all these circles overlap sits your place of purpose, the place where you will be in flow, doing what makes the most sense to you and your life.

Finding that place is a journey, and each journey starts with a first step. It's not about going there 100% tomorrow, even if that could be wonderful, I find it's more about knowing the direction, and building towards it every day.

One step at a time.

Making a plan

Rather than letting things happen, being intentional about your life journey, about what is ahead of you, helps you feel more in control as you can influence, pre-empt and prepare for events. A study found that 25% of our happiness depends on how we manage our stress,[76] and planning was the tool that worked best to manage this. Being organised and having a clear vision as to what is ahead in the long-term, but also the immediate future, is a fantastic habit to develop.

As we enter this final reflection on the impact of the pandemic, it's important to look ahead to the future. In my work, I come into contact with a diverse range of people, and this unprecedented situation has had differing consequences for all of them. And the same applies to me. I am considering what should come next. How can I emerge stronger from this period in my life, which has involved a sharper degree of change than anything that I've encountered previously? What strengths can I gain from it, and what knowledge and wisdom have I gleaned from it?

There have definitely been peaks and troughs, pain and gain, during this challenging period, but the important thing is to come out of this unenviable situation with something positive. That's something that I like to

---

[76] Harvard professor Robert Epstein,
https://en.wikipedia.org/wiki/Robert_Epstein

emphasise with my clients, the fact that even the harshest challenges can be our greatest gifts, if they help us to move forward with greater resolve and insight.

Thus, many people are reflecting on the path winding towards the horizon, contemplating the resolutions and decisions that will surface as a result of this period. And what I've noticed with many of my clients is an urge for change. They want something different.

For example, Clare, a client of mine, was suffering from Covid-19 in the very early days of the pandemic. This was a time of great uncertainty for her, as less was known about the virus back then. We had several coaching sessions around the illness itself, discussing how Covid-19 was affecting her health and mental well-being. It was an unsettling time for her, but as society began to resurface from the pandemic, something shifted. Her whole perspective on life had changed. She'd enjoyed a successful career in the corporate world, and was the Head of Marketing at an excellent sportswear company. But she decided that she wanted to do something different, something more meaningful to her. She wanted to give something back to the world and help it to heal.

After some intense and beautiful coaching sessions, she came to the decision that she wanted to assist and support people into care. She wanted to grow the medical healing side of her experience, and support people who unfortunately found themselves in vulnerable situations.

The prospect of doing something to support people was very enticing for her; it was an example of a beautiful change in circumstances that came from an initially horrible situation.

This doesn't mean that we all need to change. What is more important than change is reflection. The pandemic has represented an important opportunity to reflect on ourselves and our situation, and I hope that this book has helped catalyse this process. What you should notice is the benefit of the reflection. One of the most important skills that we develop from coaching is the raising of awareness. We understand where we are and what is here for us. Once we have developed this increased self-awareness, and awareness of our reality, we then have a responsibility to ourselves as adults to decide what we're going to do with these new insights that we've gained.

What have you learned about yourself through the pandemic?

What have you learned about yourself while reading this book ?

What's your current reality and your mindset today?

What is ahead of you?

If you project yourself in 12 months from now, what is important to you?

What will you say "yes" to?

What will you say "no" to?

What might get in the way of you progressing towards what is important to you?

How will you overcome this?

When by?

If you are pushing yourself - what are the 3 things you want to give priority to?

1st -

2nd -

3rd -

Fill in the table below:

Priorities	1st=	2nd=	3rd=
What would success look like? Be specific, think of what you would be doing and how you would feel. What would be involved etc.			
What are the key milestones on the way?			
Date of each milestone			
What is the 1st step to achieve this?			
What you will need to remember on the way.			
When will you start?			
How will you keep yourself accountable?			

Now, take a calendar, open a spreadsheet, or simply pick up a pen and paper.

Allocate these steps above against a date, organise a check in at the start of every week to see how you are getting on.

There is no perfect plan, a plan has to evolve with life, be agile, flexible and current.

Not having a plan, not knowing where you are going is the perfect recipe to meander. I strongly believe setting our intentions is the first step to any progress.

As you now know, it's not all about the doing. We can have a plan to take time off, to relax, to create space and just be. It's about creating that space with intent, whatever space that you need.

Commitment

Once you've begun to reflect on these questions and craft your answers, you have planted the seed of an idea. The next thing to consider is how you will water, fertilise and germinate your seed, so that it grows into something substantial. This will play a critical role in your ability to bounce back from this extremely testing pandemic, and from these recent months of change and challenges.

This is not necessarily an easy or quick process. It took me the best part of 8 weeks to slow down, reconnect with myself, and find my inner peace. But at a certain point, I triggered a calmness and inner joy within myself that made it possible to look ahead with purpose. This process might take longer for others, and some people might reach this place in a shorter period of time that I managed. Either is absolutely fine and normal; every journey is unique.

On reflection, what have you learned from the pandemic? What insights have you gained? What have you learned about yourself that you didn't know before? And what are you going to do about it? Doing nothing can be fine. This is a choice in itself. But it has to be a choice that suits you and suits your circumstances. Therefore, I think it's important for everyone to consider the following:

What are your post-pandemic resolutions and decisions?

What will say "yes" to going forward?

What will you create in your own life?

What will you choose to prioritise?

How will you find the strength and courage to progress with these changes?

How will you hold yourself accountable?

What do you no longer want in your life?

What are you going to push away and remove permanently from your life?

How will you make these changes stick?

If we share our resolutions with someone important to us, we are more likely to keep them. It's a well proven fact.

Who will you share your commitments to? How will you help yourself on track and progressing towards your goals?

Change takes time, effort and resilience. I am all with you, to help you bounce back and create the life you want.

As I write these final lines, I have found the strength to look up and look forward. The energy to bounce back. And I'm looking forward to the time ahead, to see what the world has to offer as we go through another period of change. Equally, I'm looking forward to working with my clients to help them achieve the same process, and identify their own purpose and meaning in their careers and lives. I feel passionate about helping people to bounce back from everything that they've been through, and to face the future with optimism.

I feel that the world is now ready to embrace more joy, more happiness, and more deep and truthful connections with one another. I am with you all on your beautiful journey.

Sincerely,

Barbara

Reflectives notes

Here is a space for you to reflect further, to journal your thoughts as they come, and to let them live on paper.

The act of journaling is healing in itself.

Use the space, dabble, experiment, draw, table, plan and try again.

We are all on a journey, finding our way. Let's enjoy it if we can.

Bibliography & Resources
To keep learning and reading

Direction / purpose

The Dare Be podcast by Gregoire Lemaitre - to get inspired by people who found fulfilment and joy in their career - https://www.darebe.me/darebepodcast

Ikigai: The Japanese secret to a long and happy life- 2017, by Héctor García and Francesc Miralles

The Boy, The Mole, The Fox and The Horse Hardcover – 2019, by Charlie Mackesy

What Color Is Your Parachute? Your Guide to a Lifetime of Meaningful Work and Career Success, 2021 by Richard N. Bolles and Katharine Brooks EdD

Positive psychology

The happiness Lab podcast by Dr Laurie Santos (Yale) -to hear share some surprising and inspiring stories that will forever alter the way you think about happiness https://www.happinesslab.fm/

Flourish: A New Understanding of Happiness and Well-Being and How To Achieve Them - 2011, by Martin Seligman

Learned Optimism: How to Change Your Mind and Your Life by - 2018, by Martin Seligman

The Little Book of Happiness: Simple Practices for a Good Life - 2019 by Miriam Akhtar

Emotional Intelligence: Why it matters more than IQ - 2020 by Daniel Goleman

Coaching

Co-Active Coaching: The proven framework for transformative conversations at work and in life - 4th edition 2018 by Henry Kimsey-House, Karen Kimsey-House, Phillip Sandahl, Laura Whitworth.

Systems Inspired Leadership: How to Tap Collective Wisdom to Navigate Change, Enhance Agility, and Foster Collaboration - 2021 by Frank Uit de Weerd and Marita Fridjhon

Coaching for Performance: The Principles and Practice of Coaching and Leadership - 2017 by Sir John Whitmore

Meditation / Inner calm

Calm, to help you meditate - https://www.calm.com/

Headspace, to help you meditate - https://www.headspace.com/

Insight timer, to meditate practice yoga and listen to Sarah Blondin https://insighttimer.com/sarahblondin

The Power of Now: A Guide to Spiritual Enlightenment - 2016 by Eckhart Tolle

Planning

The 7 Habits Of Highly Effective People: Revised and Updated - 2020, by Stephen R. Covey

The Decision Book: Fifty models for strategic thinking - 2017 by Mikael Krogerus and Roman Tschäppeler

Healing or Pandemic related

Hold Still: A Portrait of our Nation in 2020, by The Duchess of Cambridge Patron of the National Portrait Gallery and Lemn Sissay MBE 2021

Healing Is the New High: A Guide to Overcoming Emotional Turmoil and Finding Freedom, 2021 by Vex King Hay House UK.

Lunar Abundance: Cultivating Joy, Peace, and Purpose Using the Phases of the Moon

by Ezzie Spencer PhD | 29 Mar 2018

Mind. (2020). The mental health emergency: How has the coronavirus pandemic impacted our mental health?

Acknowledgements

Thank you to my amazing and inspiring clients and friends - who were brave to ask for help when they needed it. I am truly grateful for every minute with them, and for this wonderful profession, which took some time and soul searching to find.

Thank you Chris for your fantastic research and expertise, I could not have done this without you.

Thank you Greg, I love your faith in me and how every day you encourage me to be the better version of myself. Thank you to my children, from whom and with whom I learn everyday. Louise your feedback was a true blessing, it gave me the willpower to keep pushing when I was giving up. My dear friends and family who have been supporting me through this year of writing - thank you from the bottom of my heart. Thank you to my parents who taught me that anything is possible if you set your heart (and mind) to it.

About the Author

Barbara is a certified professional coach (CPCC and PCC), team coach & and coach trainer. During the last few years she has worked with hundreds of clients to help them bounce back in a meaningful way. She works globally as a facilitator, inspirational speaker and coach. Her approach is holistic - using a combination of emotional literacy and action-driven objectives that encourages her clients to go deep and think beyond their traditional framework.

Barbara is currently an Associate Board Member for the UK Chapter of the International Coaching Federation. Previously she was solicitor, a headhunter for the top global strategy firms, an entrepreneur, and part of Google campus in London. She has lived and worked in Singapore, Germany, France and in the UK, with her husband and 3 wonderful children. Outside of her coaching passion, Barbara loves to spend time with her family and friends over a never-ending French meal and to spin her pottery wheel with her children.

Follow her on social media-

Instagram @bouncingbackbook and @dare.be.me

LinkedIn @BarbaraDewast

Printed in Great Britain
by Amazon